Dear Erika,

LEAN ON!

Thanks a lot for supporting my book! there are many who think but a lot less who act. I respect you for acting on your goodwill and being a true friend.

I wish you a successful life and career, with my book getting to play a part in all that you achieve...

Take care!

Mohit

LEAN ON!

EVOLUTION OF OPERATIONS
EXCELLENCE WITH DIGITAL
TRANSFORMATION IN
MANUFACTURING AND BEYOND

MOHIT GUPTA

NEW DEGREE PRESS

LEAN ON!

EVOLUTION OF OPERATIONS EXCELLENCE WITH DIGITAL

TRANSFORMATION IN MANUFACTURING AND BEYOND

ISBN   978-1-63676-847-2   *Paperback*

                978-1-63730-195-1   *Kindle Ebook*

                978-1-63730-291-0   *Ebook*

To Mom, Dad, and Smriti
Friends, Mentors, and my Sensei
who have been my constant
source of inspiration.

And to the almighty for His blessings.

CONTENTS

CHAPTER I

HOW TO USE THIS BOOK

———

This book is an exploration of process design in different industries. I start with the history and go over a few very important tools explained through stories and ending at the various possibilities of evolution of the Lean process. I expect my readers to be students who want to enter the fascinating world of operations and manufacturing, professionals who are already there and need to explore deeper, or just enthusiasts of lean.

Students should use it for learning the brief history of Lean and enjoy a few actual stories that people dealt with while implementing lean. I imagined myself being in that position as a second-year engineering student, but I hardly had a book introducing me to the concept of lean from scratch. I have made sure that I introduce every Japanese word that you hear for the first time in this book in the form of a story that you can relate with.

The stories will also be something that you would come across in your professional life at least once. I would urge you to refer the list of resources mentioned at the end of the book to relate to the topics better and get a better understanding of the subject. There are some interesting podcasts out there that I would want you to leverage while you enjoy this book. Students who are engineers should start from the first chapter to get the basics and the right context to understand the stories in the subsequent chapters.

For professionals, unless you are comfortable with the basic tools of Lean (multiple websites claim to have twenty-five "top Lean tools" that organizations deploy), skip the first two chapters—they describe the basic terms in the form of small anecdotes I collected from different interviews as well as my own experiences. Use them to calibrate your experience with mine... I would love to listen to your stories if you want to connect with me personally!

Enthusiasts—you are the special ones. You have a lot of curiosities and I have made an attempt to cater to those in this book. I compare things, answer many myths, and talk about real incidents to explain the evolution of Lean over time for many of the operations leaders that I spoke with. I hope you use this book as yet another way to enter the future and create your own opinions as an operations enthusiast like me.

Now, let's begin.

CHAPTER (II)

INTRODUCTION

———

It was a cold day in October 2019. I was sitting in a conference room when I was taken aback with how the host ordered the group a cup of coffee. He never moved an inch and instead uttered the magic words: "Alexa, make me a cup of coffee." Hearing the coffee machine whirring on his commands was the next thing that blew me away. I was in "tech shock." We have all seen the evolution of the humble doorbell. It has evolved from alerting the homeowner of a visitor at the door to a futuristic mobile-controlled, video-enabled *Ring*, which provides an array of convenience and security features.[1] These are examples of new technology that has disrupted the way people conduct their daily lives. In fact, the technologies represent quantum shifts in how people interact with the world today.

As a mechanical engineer, I see and think about all the components and the way the products function as well as the *mechanics* behind all these marvels. I wonder about the

---

1. Taylor Soper, Nat Levy, "Amazon to Acquire Ring Video Doorbell Maker, Cracking Open the Door in Home Security Market," *GeekWire*, February 27, 2018.

processes that might be used to enable the disruptions in examples above. How did we decide one day that we needed a video assistance on our entrance? How did the creators connect that design vision to the actual product? There must be some changes in the way these products were built—changes which could make the time-to-market of those products faster or control the quality variation of each unit of the product. A drastic reduction in the timeline of a product launch means that they have acquired a lot of agility in how they were built. These developments have a pattern that seems to occur every twenty years.

To understand how the present products are made, I dove deeper and contacted my friend, who proudly carries the electric vehicle baton in a start-up based in the west coast of the United States. He has led operations in companies like Tesla and General Electric and currently wears the operations hat at an underwater AV company. Due to COVID-19, the production at his company slowed down. He saw this as an opportunity and managed to convince the founder of the company that they should rebuild their manufacturing processes from top to bottom. He stressed the importance of this overhaul because a company cannot expect to keep releasing "upgrades" in the product without ceasing to "upgrade" the inherent process used to make the product. That's why he is happy. He knows customers have crazy expectations and to keep pace with them, the company needs to be a step ahead. So, he has taken a step back to create standard defect-free processes to build the basics right, which will help his company continuously improve.

On the flip side, the founder of the company, like every entrepreneur, worries about growth and returns. He believes that the team needs to prove the product's value before thinking about stopping and improving. To him, stopping production means losing potential sales.

I have seen this clash of thoughts before. I have explored and tried to question these clashes in my interviews with many operations leaders. To my surprise, I was able to resolve a lot of doubts that I had in comparing the businesses in the US and worldwide. Not to give away much, but one of the things that I discovered is that continuous improvement and optimized production are, inherently, forms of art and need to be paid special attention.

World View

Elon Musk says, "Humans are underrated."[2] There is nothing that humans cannot conquer. We like to think logically and structure our thoughts based on our past experiences. Think of the impact of a process defect today. For a typical automotive manufacturer, the cost of an unplanned downtime is over $1.3 million per hour, or $361 per second. So, if an employee spends three minutes calling a supervisor about a breakdown, they have spent $65,000 just to let someone know that that they have a problem. Over the years, Lean has triumphed in establishing mechanisms to avoid such failures and ensuring a foolproof process to avoid another failure to occur.[3]

The initial mechanical tools used from the Industrial Revolution of 1700s, for the next one hundred and fifty years are termed Industry 1.0, which was nothing but the manual

---

2. Katie Roof, "Elon Musk Says, 'Humans are Underrated,' Calls Tesla's 'Excessive Automation' a 'Mistake'," TechCrunch, April 13, 2018.

3. "State of Things | Smart Manufacturing (Part 3): Use Case Modelling," Enterprise IoT Insights, accessed September 8, 2020.

creation of value.[4] The 1920s saw the start of mass production in the manufacturing industry in the US. This was Industry 2.0. Mass production had begun with increased demand from domestic business as well as the World Wars. A company producing thousands of products daily inspired shock and awe. But this trend evolved differently in the East and the West. While the United States focused on increasing production, Japan focused on increasing efficiency. Following Japan's success, the United States quickly shifted from mass production to improving quality and efficiency.

Robotics was at the heart of efficiency for the most part of the 1950s until the 1980s. This was Industry 3.0. It was all mechanical but still helped in doing jobs in conditions that humans could not—high temperatures and deep seas. Now with the onset of thetwenty-first century, we are in Industry 4.0.[5] Almost everyone has created the capability to manufacture with accuracy and precision. A lot of credit for this goes to robots and to the new ways of using data. Today, success in manufacturing relies on the data generated in production and how we integrate the different steps in the value chain to create efficiency.

The Problem

Lean came into existence when organizations required efficiency in business. You become "lean" when you shed fat. For businesses, wasteful resource utilization is the "fat" that needs to be shed. Six Sigma came into being to support organized

---

4. "Industrial Revolution—From Industry 1.0 to Industry 4.0," Desoutter Tools, accessed September 8, 2020.

5. Ibid.

problem resolution. Six Sigma is a way to measure the variation in our processes and is one of the famous quality tools used in every industry. Lean and Six Sigma are now common names in manufacturing and are used interchangeably. Managers do a simple improvement and claim to have made their processes "lean." In reality, these projects are more complex with many new and unique break points. Creating complex process system improvements requires time and patience to be successful. This path is excruciatingly slow and requires investment that not many companies are prepared to make.

In this book, I set out to see how Lean can be used in a new era of digital transformation for different industries that flips norms on their heads. The global manufacturing value affected by digital transformation is over $10 trillion, aided by many supporting factors. The cost of sensors and virtualization of manufacturing has been reduced one hundred times in the last decade. Digital transformation impacts the traditional design process. My friend who shifted three electric vehicle companies saw the same trend in all of them. There is now more focus on automation, product testing, and simulations. These attributes are still not discussed widely in Lean manufacturing. Rather, many operations leaders suffer because the adopters of Lean overlook this crucial philosophy when they are rapidly expanding.

So, the company CEOs and, subsequently, the operations leaders need help. Process design is too fragmented and falls prey to the pretty technology. Software programs have been developed over their own platform of "Agile." Agile is a distant relative of Lean that got developed in the software world.[6] The world without Agile was linear. Software

6.   "What is Agile?," Agile Alliance, accessed September 8, 2020.

used to be developed in a sequential chain, handing over the developed product from one step to the next. Agile helped to create multiple iterations of the same product to reduce the lead time in developing the product.

But what happens when Agile meets Lean? What happens when more software engineers are developing a physical product than traditional design engineers? What changes will Six Sigma undergo with the future of work? The smarter companies are faster adopters and practice smarter implementation.

According to *Forbes*, 70 percent of the companies either have a digital strategy or are working on one to transform their operations.[7] Companies see how going digital can bring them a brighter future. Developing apps and creating digital documentation are also on the rise because most technology companies are undergoing some form of tech-transition. A robust plan starts with defining a process, which provides a foundation for a complete digital transformation.

Why Read This Book?

This book, predominantly, discusses the problem of evolution of Lean processes with digital transformation. I have been supported by active operations leaders who share their perspective with me. Many times, it is those leaders who give me different avenues to discuss the idea of digital solutions in manufacturing and grassroot operations.

This book also describes a possible confluence between the two worlds—physical and digital—where the proven

---

7. "100 Stats on Digital Transformation and Customer Experience," *Forbes*, accessed September 8, 2020.

process of Lean meets the software process of Agile. I have relentlessly tried to uncover these differences and make what Lean should be today— seamless with the digital world.

I'm an explorer here. An explorer who loves putting his inquisitiveness to good use by learning stories about things beyond my normal reach. Those who know me from school times know my reputation of sharing notes with fellow students to help them in their examination blues. This is what I am trying to do in this book. I have traded places from being a student who crams and regurgitates to being a researcher who asks and ponders. I ask many questions that I break down further along with a lot of people in this book to give you the Lean of the future. In my journey to explore the merger of physical and digital Lean, I talked to a lot of people who are unsung heroes of their companies. They have optimized and polished operational processes countless times. Lean is slow, hence most of their heroics go unnoticed.

My intention with this book is to explore. I see it as a perfect fit for an engineer who is curious about the manufacturing space and its realities. This book is for the professional entering into manufacturing and wants to have a crash course on how they can set up their work for success. It is also for an entrepreneur looking for ways to optimize business operations, or a curious business leader trying to break free from the traditional ways of operational excellence. I seek curious readers looking to educate themselves about technology and the future of work.

This is what will revolutionize the future. To me, we are at an inflection point where products are being eaten by software. But what if Lean eats software? This is a logical next step in understanding the future of Lean manufacturing in the era of digital transformation.

Another thing is knowing about Lean for service industries. I attempt to venture into these industries from IT teams to supply chains, from start-ups to government offices, looking for Lean. Many things that you interact with nowadays have some hidden Lean examples. A popular example is Gordon Ramsay, who turns around failing restaurants on his show *Kitchen Nightmares*.[8] He uses Lean to shorten the menus and connect the owners with their inherently excellent dishes. Digital check-ins or a kiosk at an airport entrance are other examples. These systems cut down wait times and make the process leaner. Marie Kondo rose to the occasion of cleaning and organizing people's homes by using a set of Lean tools.

Examples of digital world supporting processes are also everywhere now. However, it is better to know those examples from leaders who deal with them every day, isn't it? If you want to learn from the operations leaders and Lean practitioners around the globe, read on!

---

8.   *Kitchen Nightmares*, "Fine Dining is a Fine Mess | Kitchen Nightmares," January 27, 2021, video, 4:10.

CHAPTER III

MY INSPIRATION STORY

———

Books have been a love of mine for a long time. I belong to a family of PhDs and have always striven to provide them with my excellence in this field by being at the top of my class.

For the past fifteen years, I have pursued academics more than anything else. All my student life, I have been a bookworm, but only confined to my textbooks. Maybe that makes me a textbook-loving bookworm. My dad has a huge library at home, a separate room dedicated to books, mostly spiritual ones and science non-fictions. I still remember my middle school days when my dad redid the whole room and I helped him organize it, book by book on the shelves. It covered the whole wall at the back of his big brown table and a recliner executive chair. Entering the room, I used to wonder: How do you read so many books? My academic mind was tuned to remember, or rather cram stuff up in my brain, to a point that I could regurgitate everything word by word. But this had to change someday.

This room posed a challenge to me. My dad, ever a scholar, was using his time to get to know more about the various perspectives of science and spirituality. He is always like that.

Books are his way to shape his point of view better. What I lacked was the patience and hunger to go beyond my set lines. Or so I thought. My trained student brain was accustomed to start from one end and eat up all the words instead of understanding the stories. My dad was on the opposite end of me, understanding the books instead of memorizing them. He became my instant hero for reading so many books and being able to *remember* all of them.

Then came a time when I became an engineer and, like a solid Indian techie, I was ready to face the real world. As they say, the real world is not a set of fairy tales and is definitely not run by a book of rules. I understood this fact quickly as I was faced with challenges demanding knowledge and application more than "remembering" formulae. I took this challenge with both hands and chased my dreams of making breakthrough improvements in the automobile industry and joined one of the largest automotive companies in India, Tata Motors, to work and learn.

The year 2017 will remain special for me just because of the way it added wings to my craving to go beyond the book knowledge. It was also the time I met with a special mentor who guided me toward a new way of learning. It was a form of tough love, so to speak. I was a new team member on a million-dollar project. The first task for me was to learn the Japanese concepts on the assembly line, which he was leading. As my first assignment after that training, I was expected to learn those concepts and teach it within two weeks to my team of ninety-five operators. The way I learnt things here was 80 percent practical and just 20 percent theory. I quickly realized that if I wanted to train my team of operators, I would need to absorb the concepts and explain them in the simplest language possible. In a matter of days, I felt so much lighter and agile while learning, doing, and teaching at the same time. Very soon, the company went into a restructuring mode and while I was training to understand these concepts and enjoying the brief student life, I shifted away from the shopfloor and moved to a more corporate role. At this point, I had already realized that I belonged to the field. I took a deeper dive into learning on the ground while trying to understand the concepts even though, in this new role, I sat in front of a laptop in an airconditioned office.

It was here when my new boss, Mr. Anal Singh, who was the manufacturing head of the facility, inspired me to question everything I saw on the assembly line and link it with what I learned from the Japanese training. As a manufacturing head, he had a daily routine of picking up a shop and doing an impromptu visit to inspect the teams. He would never talk to the manager first. Instead, he would wait at a work-station and would look at the work done by an operator. He would be ready with a list of improvement points to talk about how the operator could bring his toolbox closer, improve on his posture, increase his speed of work, or add a quality checkpoint after his job. That was the magic of his twenty-seven-year-old trained and experienced eyes. He would then share the feedback with the manager, sometimes days later, in an executive meeting.

This changed my perspective of my new "corporate role" completely. I used to get inspired by his tireless routine and would travel a lot with him in different production setups as well as supplier workshops to learn more and to increase my inquisitiveness on the processes I saw. I started loving the interactions with the line foreman or supervisors in understanding how they designed their process controls and managed their teams to hit the target every day, every hour, and to the minute.

Turning profits at a company like Tata was not easy. It is a behemoth, and one needs to be patient to understand the scale of work that goes on every day. It took me two years to get my first taste of big success. I used all my learnings to provide a $200,000 annual savings to the company through a host of cost reduction projects. While doing this project, I partnered with a team of McKinsey consultants. I would share my process knowledge with them, and they would come up with ideas for cost reduction. Some of the solutions were so easy that I used to think the amount of money we could've saved if those solutions were done earlier. By this time, I was fortunate to get a level up in my learning and also got to see the business aspect of the company. After we finished the project, I started believing that imparting knowledge to your team is the most valuable work that a professional can do.

I resolved to be a subject matter expert in Lean Six Sigma. I wanted to explore more about Lean processes but would always end up reading a random newsletter or a blog. It was then when I brought up the idea of writing a book with one of my friends. At the time it was in jest, but somewhere in my mind, I knew that it was dearly needed! My friend pushed me to go beyond automobiles and think about the next revolution of IoT and Industry 4.0 in other fields. I got inspired by Tesla in those days and decided to follow this next revolution by coming to the US, starting with my MBA.

My time in the US has been a dream come true. As an MBA student, I was thrown in a pool of multiple domains, people with diverse backgrounds and a cocktail of available career paths, multiple functions, and new experiences.

Suddenly the whole world was open to venture. One year into the program, I became nostalgic and called up my boss to catch up with him and share with him the new world that I had discovered coming out of India for the first time ever. He was happy to hear about my progress but, as a force of his old habits, he shared something very new for me to ponder. The company had started working on automating the vehicles and was suddenly filled with an array of programmers and project managers alongside the traditional research and development team that it had. It posed a challenge for the manufacturing team to deal with a list of new automated systems added in the vehicles, which before were limited to a humble set of sensors and an electronic control unit.

He was worried about the change in process structures that it would bring to the plant. It meant uprooting the system that I built on the foundations of Lean for over two years and replacing it with Scrum and Agile to include software development in many parts of the vehicle (Don't get hung up on the words now—they are different techniques that I will talk about in the subsequent chapters. For now, consider them as two process design brothers: one with a cool hoodie on, coding on the computer, and the other wearing overalls, working on the shop floor).

So, for my boss, it meant two parallel systems—a physical system of waterfall and Agile for software development—working together to build one product. He was aware of both systems, but it seemed to be huge work for the mechanical team under him to digest this change. I was intrigued yet not surprised by this new development. I had seen this happen in the US with at least twenty-one new companies working on autonomous vehicles and the drones for last mile deliveries. I realized this was the best time to explore the missing pieces of the new digital revolution by getting to know the stories of professionals in the world of operations. It would also give me a chance to rendezvous with my old friend, Lean.

My affection with Lean knows no bounds, and I have carried it with me even to the US to see where it all applies. With an exposure to industries like healthcare, retail, hospitality, social impact, and finance, I realized that this concept of Lean can be placed in every field with slight changes. Lean is also a tool which is bound to undergo a lot of business changes with healthcare changing to telehealth, retail changing to e-commerce, and finance changing to fintech.

I am as new to this world as you are, but my attempt is to reach out to the leaders and compile the possibilities of the future in making this as seamless for the digital world as possible. I have traded places from being a student who crams and regurgitates to a researcher who asks and ponders. I have come full circle, realizing that learning is not just about memorizing and regurgitating information. Rather, it is a constant acquisition of knowledge done by thinking deeply, applying concepts, and asking the right questions.

PART 1

CHAPTER 1

LEAN | HIGHLIGHTS FROM THE PAST

—

Did you know that the idea for Lean came from slaughterhouses?[9] When Henry Ford was creating Model T, he discovered Lean after studying animal disassembly at a meatpacking plant in Chicago. Many developments took place before we got to a point of adopting this gem as a standard practice. Before diving into Mr. Ford's story, let's take a step back and understand the Industrial Revolution through just one factor: geographical reach.

The Origin

Without transportation, communities couldn't ship and sell goods. India couldn't share its spices, and China couldn't sell its silk. Prior to the expansion of railroads, most trade

---

9. Mark Graban, "A Lean Slaughterhouse?," *Lean Blog* (blog), Last Updated Dec 12, 2012.

relied on ships, which is why major cities grew up beside large bodies of water.[10]

The landscape of our civilization changed with the expansion of better modes of transportation. Gradually, international trade prospered. This increased the demand for goods everywhere, which pressured manufacturers to produce more goods in less time. The creation of machines spurred the first Industrial Revolution. By the mid-nineteenth century, manufacturing in major parts of the United States and the United Kingdom had started using the concepts of division of labor, machine-assisted manufacturing, and assembly of standardized parts.[11] The growth of manufacturing was accelerated by the rapid expansion of rail, ship, and road transportation. Let's see a few ingredients of the process and break them into different components to see how each of them evolved with time.

The first thing we need to define is "what" of an operations process. A process requires three main components. First, there are the actors: the people who do a task. Second, the machines: the tools and equipment which the actors use to complete their tasks. And third, the management: the managers who work to achieve bigger goals of producing and selling a product and eventually earning a profit. An easy way to divide processes is to treat them as actions that are sandwiched between an input and an output.

The second ingredient of operations is "why?" Everything that a company does revolves around two goals. First, to reduce the costs of its input and processes, and second, to increase the quality of its output. Cost and quality have

---

10. "Assembly Line," *Science*, Accessed August 10, 2020.

11. Ibid.

been used to evaluate a company's performance for a very long time. Manufacturers ventured to create the power loom and steam engine technologies to add a third component: time to make a product. But it did not stop there. The beast of industrial revolution had to be controlled, especially the quality of the products, which could go out of hand with faster production. While the equipment had mechanized, the performance of workers was yet to be upgraded. There was still a huge gap of using those machines efficiently.[12]

Two major developments in the 1870s and 1880s attempted to bridge this gap. The first used scientific studies on processes. In the United States, three pioneers paved the way to study processes closely and create a foundation for manufacturing industry to follow. They were Frederick Taylor and Frank and Lillian Gilbreth. They started studying manufacturing processes in separate parts of the United States.[13]

Frank and Lillian Gilbreth pioneered the study of movements used by workers to complete their processes. The Gilbreths observed the process and then broke down the motions into micro-motions and measured them in seconds. This simple process, which could be compared and improved repeatedly, came to be known as time and motion studies. In the Gilbreth's biographical novel, *Cheaper by The Dozen*, the couple tries to apply their efficiency methods in their household of twelve children. Frank Gilbreth tried to instill excellence in everything that he taught his kids. His intelligence and devotion to excellence engender a great deal of respect in all the people who know him. One day when one of his kids, Anne, disobeyed him and complained that she

---

12. A Brief History of Lean," Lean Enterprise Institute, accessed August 10, 2020.

13. Ibid.

was not respected by her classmates because they considered her a freak, he told her, "No person with inner dignity is ever embarrassed."[14] He regarded all kinds of work to be the same and tried to champion them by finding the best way to do each one of them.

On the other hand, in his pursuit to excellence, Frederick Taylor studied the way workers moved while doing tasks like moving material or shoveling. He then designed methods that would reduce the effort of the workers. In his book, *The Principles of Scientific Management,* Taylor discusses four principles of scientifically distributing work among workers and managers. He proposed selecting, training, and providing detailed instructions to each worker to assess performance and develop repetitive actions that would eliminate defects. His idea in his own words is that "the remedy for this inefficiency lies in systematic management, rather than in searching for some unusual or extraordinary man."[15]

Both pioneers created the organizational structure of many manufacturing operations. While century-old theories may not seem to be applicable in today's fast-paced, technology-driven world, process designs still use a similar structure to define and standardize both manual and robotic motions today. In an interview that I conducted with a Lean consultant who has seen these developments for over thirty years, he says, "the base of Lean is managing culture and discipline. Everything else that you see are the tools and will change in every generation."

---

14. Anonymous, *Reading: Taylor and the Gilbreths*, (Lumen Learning: Pressbooks), accessed August 10, 2020.

15. Frank B. Gilberth and Ernestine Gilberth Carey, *Cheaper by the Dozen*, (New York: Thomas Y. Crowell Co., 1948).

The second development occurred in the 1910s in Detroit, Michigan. Henry Ford set a goal for his company: "A motor car for the great magnitude." Automobiles were expensive, custom-made machines at that time, so Ford's goal was ambitious. He set out to produce a simple, less expensive mass-produced car for a wider consumer base.[16] He and his team used four principles to further their goal: use interchangeable parts, develop a continuous flow, divide the labor, and reduce wasted effort.

Ford started his crusade for the people's car in 1907 by developing processes to increase the productivity of his workers. His production of the Ford Model T started in 1908, but it still took over twelve hours to produce. He spent five years fine tuning the manufacturing and standardizing parts for the car. In 1913, he discovered methods used by grain-mill conveyors and meat-packing plants in Chicago. The slaughterhouses used monorail trolleys to move suspended carcasses past a line of stationary workers, each of whom did one specific task. He started applying this conveyor method for aggregate parts like fender and panels. Then came the pièce de résistance: a conveyor for assembling the complete vehicle. The Ford team developed the first moving assembly line in large-scale manufacturing. Now making cars at a record-breaking rate, he could lower the price and still make a good profit by selling more cars. The assembly line transformed the organization of work, and by the end of World War I, the principle of continuous movement was sweeping mass-production industries of the world, soon to become an integral part of modern industry.[17]

---

16. Goodreads, "Cheaper by the Dozen Quotes," accessed January 10, 2021.
17. "A Brief History of Lean," Lean Enterprise Institute, accessed August 10, 2020.

The basic elements of traditional assembly line methods are nearly all the same. First, the sequence in which a product's component parts are put together must be planned and designed into the process. Then the first manufactured component passes from station to station, often by conveyor belt, with work done in each station. By the last station, the fully assembled product is identical to each one before and after it. This system produces large quantities of uniform-quality goods at a relatively low cost.

Ford had another innovative idea: his workers were also potential consumers. In 1914, Ford workers' wages were raised to five dollars a day—a wage high enough to allow employees to buy their own Model Ts! Ford was called "a traitor to his class" by other industrialists and professionals, but he held firm in believing that well-paid workers tolerate dull work and are loyal—and buy his cars. "That," he said, "is the best kind of cost reduction I can do."[18]

Ford brought together consistently interchangeable parts with standard work and conveyors to create what he called flow production. From the standpoint of a manufacturing engineer, however, the breakthroughs went much further.

Continuing Ford's Methods

Henry Ford produced the Model T until 1927. By that time, he had produced fifteen million vehicles in fourteen years. However, many things needed improvement, namely variety.[19] Consumers wanted additional features in their beloved cars.

---

18. Ibid.
19. "Ford installs first moving assembly line 1913," PBS, accessed August 10, 2020.

At the time, a famous saying would go for Model T: "You can have any color you want—as long as it's black!" The reason was simple—all the cars had to be identical, and black was the only color available. This uniformity kept production output high and avoided complications from product complexities. Ford agreed to this challenge but said that it would take a village to add a different model on the same conveyor belt and still run equally efficiently.

On the other side of globe in Japan, Kiichiro Toyoda and Taiichi Ohno had found the solution to the shortcomings in Ford's production in Japan. By 1923, they devised advanced methods to take care of irregularities caused by multi-model lines and created what we today know as Toyota Production System (TPS). The system shifted the focus from an individual machine's utilization to the flow of product through the total process. TPS was created to bring discipline to the processes and stability at its foundation.[20]

I respect TPS because of its simplicity and customer-centric nature. The first of its two pillars is just-in-time (JIT) processing, which tells the manufacturer to produce products only when requested by the customer. The second pillar called autonomation, or *Jidoka*, which means adding intelligent automation to keep things faster and safer. In other words, TPS streamlined the flow of any kind of "value-add," whether tangible or intangible.

A little-known fact is that Toyota got its inspiration for its production system from the United States. A few years after the second world war, a delegation from Toyota visited the United States to study its commercial enterprises. They visited an American supermarket, Piggly Wiggly, and observed

---

20. Ibid.

that staff reordered and restocked the items only when those items were purchased. This gave them the idea of *Kanban,* a system that relies on JIT processing, which is central to TPS.[21] I'll explain this term in detail in the next chapter.

An example of TPS in action is Apple's launch of the iPhone 11, 11 Pro, and 11 Pro-Max in 2019. Each model is also available with various storage capacities, colors, and other options. To quench the thirst of Apple-nerds, the company would need something like TPS to optimize its costs while producing all the models in large volumes. Specifically, the two pillars of TPS suggested the following:

1. A unit is produced only when the customer orders one. This creates a "pull" in the system to produce only what is required as opposed to a "push" system where Apple creates a large supply of iPhones in every color and feature and then expects to sell them.[22]
2. As a part of *Jidoka*, the flow of material and assembly of the phone is the quickest and most efficient way to deliver the phone to the customer. The system should ensure that each phone is defect-free and made from lowest costs.

Where We Are Now

One of the operations leaders that I interviewed remarked, "TPS had brought companies a long way, but its

---

21. Laquita Harris, "Lean Manufacturing Made Toyota the Success Story it is Today," RCBI, April 2008.
22. Leonardo Group Americas, "How Piggly Wiggly Revolutionized Manufacturing, or the Quite Genius of a Milk Rack," *Medium*, Feb 04, 2015.

implementation has introduced more challenges and more solutions." Once the manufacturing plants over the world started implementing TPS, productivity increased, and costs decreased. However, the nature of work in a factory changed radically. Skilled workers were replaced by semi-skilled or even unskilled workers because tasks had been minutely compartmentalized, so each worker assembled or added one particular part. Manufacturers soon realized that not only were a great number of managers and supervisors required to oversee these laborers, but a high degree of pre-planning on their part was also essential. Overall, operations became more complex and required correct sequencing.[23]

The product and the assembly line had to be designed before assembly line production could begin. The simpler tasks focused on customer delight and this became more critical to its success. The simple, straightforward assembly line became a highly complex process designed in smaller chunks. There are some big examples in this area that underlined this change: wholesale stores like IKEA started using simple visual aids like floor tapes for safer and easier access to customers, and supply chains divided up their work into minute details and got high efficiencies in areas like inventory management.[24] Walmart is one such example of a company putting in huge resources in process mapping and inventory management across stores by using big data.

In the 1980s and 1990s, the robotics revolution created another transition in manufacturing. While the Toyota Production System gained popularity in the West, electronics became the second major industry to adopt the concept. In

23. Manu Joy, "Lean Leadership," Researchgate, April 2019.
24. Mike Wilson, "Going Lean: IKEA style," February 21, 2013.

the United States, Motorola took the baton from Toyota in manufacturing. New innovations in Lean enterprises moved away from machines to electronic technology. Motorola also started another concept, Six Sigma. While TPS was built around the manufacturing processes in a factory, the electronic industry emphasized management as well. Six Sigma is a management technique built off of mass production principles with more focus on minimizing variability. Six Sigma principles reduced cycle time, pollution, and costs while increasing customer satisfaction and profits. This evolved into a process called "Lean Six Sigma."[25]

An interesting change happened in the tools used under Lean Six Sigma. Earlier, TPS defined seven types of wastes: transportation, inventory, motion, waiting, overproduction, over-processing, and defects, which are known as TIMWOOD.[26] All seven were targeted to improve processes. Lean Six Sigma added an eighth one: non-utilized talent. Talent is mostly overlooked in the process of identifying waste in operations. This addition checked whether the company is utilizing all potential skills of the employees. It represents a shift from improving processes to improving management.

The third and final shift brings us up to date. In the 2000s, internet and software industries boomed. Before, during, and after the dot-com bubble, the internet industries did not use many Lean principles or optimize their resources because they were all backed by venture capitalists. Software development needed to be Agile as users and new features rapidly evolved with every product. In February 2001, a manifesto

---

25. "The 8 Wastes of Lean—Stop Wasting Your Resources," *Leanscape* (blog), August 20, 2020, accessed August 25, 2020.

26. Ibid.

was created to align software development processes using standard processes. It was aptly called the Agile Manifesto.[27]

Along with the Agile software movement, companies, especially start-ups, applied both Lean and Agile software principles to develop new products efficiently, based on validated customer demand. Early practices of Lean enterprise and Agile software principles were commonly referred to as Lean start-ups. After almost twenty years of that manifesto and the evolution of the Lean start-up, the physical and digital overlap in many ways.

What are these overlaps? How does the digital factor become so important in the past few years? Which areas become challenging for the leaders to understand, implement, and impact their bottom line? These are some questions that warrant stories from different industries and will define the future path for operations excellence. I talk about such challenges in the chapters to come. But before that, let's look at some Lean terms that might have troubled you while reading this chapter.

---

27. Agile Manifesto, "History: The Agile Manifesto," Accessed August 10, 2020.

CHAPTER 2

HORS D'OEUVRE | STORIES ON LEAN JARGON

This section is dedicated to the readers who wish to brush up their understanding of the normal jargon words used in the book quite often. I have connected a story to each jargon to explain them in the most practical manner and also share with you how I got acquainted with them.

Kaizen

Kaizen is a Japanese word that means "change for the better." Any action that is performed on the production line to cause a performance improvement is termed as a *Kaizen* for the area. On a shop floor, you'll hear this word synonymous to "progress." If your manager wants you to create and execute some improvement projects, there is a high chance, he or she will refer to a "*Kaizen* event." In most process-improvement setups, a *Kaizen* event is a well-structured and organized activity where subject matter experts and cross-functional team members gather and solve a problem by going to its root cause and eliminating it in a set timeline.[28] It involves a bunch of documents, and the efficacy of the solution is tracked until a permanent solution is found. A *Kaizen* event ensures that said issue or problem never occurs again.

You can view *Kaizen* as all incremental changes you do in any area of your work that make it easy for you to come back and start quicker. You are new to the company and drive first day to the office taking "Route A." Next day, you find another route, "Route B," which is ten minutes faster. Voila! You just did a *Kaizen* on your driving route. You are managing your daily meetings and find that creating a ten-minute huddle in the morning can save you an hour's worth of team emails every day. That's another *Kaizen*. On the other extreme, you have two robot machines working at 50 percent efficiency in your shop floor. You assemble your team and manage to combine the work on a single robot. That's a *Kaizen* saving you thousands of dollars.

Another defining characteristic of *Kaizen* is that it relies heavily on employee feedback, rather than customer or client feedback. Most of the suggested improvements in a *Kaizen* environment come directly from workers in the organization. This is beneficial to businesses, as they face less resistance when implementing requested improvements and changes driven from bottom to top. It's intended to be embedded into your organization's corporate culture as a way of day-to-day operating.

---

28. Sarah K. White, "What is Kaizen? A Business Strategy Focused on Improvement," *CIO*, July 16, 2019.

5S

5S stands for *Seiri, Seiton, Seiso, Seiketsu, Shitsuke.* These five words translate in English as "sort", "set in order", "shine", "standardize," and "sustain" respectively.[29] This is the first step to every improvement. This is similar to how your parents tell you to start your day with making your bed and keeping your room clean before you start studying or doing any other constructive activity. It is simple, basic, and, surprisingly, the most overlooked phase of the whole process. 5S enhances visual management. Anyone can see a visually-improved area and exclaim, "Well it looks different, so there must be some problems solved in this area." While Lean consultants start with 5S to create an impression, they haven't even started with addressing the actual problem. It is similar to just putting a dress on a pig. It is now a well-dressed pig, but it is still a pig!

While I was working at Tata, a new graduate engineering trainee (also called a GET) in the manufacturing division would be given 5S as their first task on the shop floor. I started as a GET at Tata and out of the five different workshops present in that factory, I was assigned the general assembly line. It was the place where the painted metal bodies of pickup-trucks used to drop and where all the functional and aesthetic parts from seats to tires and engine used to get fitted over forty plus workstations. Each station was operated by a number of associates. At first, I used to gaze at the speed with which the associates used to work at their assigned station. The most complex task on the line was laying out electrical

---

29. "What are the Five Ss (5S) of Lean," American Society for Quality, accessed September 9, 2020.

wiring for the complete car. You could see even that kind of task getting completed within three minutes! Rather, that was the speed of the complete line. Every three minutes, a pickup up truck would roll off of the line!

I was asked to inspect the area and look for any 5S "violations" or opportunities of improvement. I used to walk up and down the whole forty-stations-long assembly line for a bunch of 5S-audits with my team. At that time, the task would look really fun and simple. I identified some specific spots that I knew remained messy all the time. To me, 5S meant recognizing the areas that were not orderly, and I would take pictures of the mess and report them back. I would feel like an examination invigilator ensuring that no one was cheating, where I wouldn't really have to give an exam. But that joy was short-lived.

Little did I know that my boss was collecting them, visiting those places himself, and then putting me in charge to improve those same areas. That was my first *Kaizen* event, so to speak. 5S suddenly became my worst enemy. Haha!

The key to this tool is the last S, *Shitsuke*, which is sustaining your improvement forever. And, like a class teacher who knows that there are kids in the class who are sincere and there are others who will never listen to her, I knew that there were some messed up corners in that shop. Those same spots that I had very cheerfully identified before were now being taken care by some "kids" who would never listen to my lecture on cleanliness and 5S. It used to be a combination of providing incentives and investing on bins and tools that would automatically make the area more organized for them. However, this first task of 5S given by my boss later came in use for my further explorations with visual management and standardization of work in the shop.

Kanban

Kanban is a term associated with supply chain. But lately, it has become a fundamental tool for Agile practitioners, too. *Kanban* gets its name from the use of visual signaling mechanisms to control work in progress for intangible work products (*Kanban* = card you can see). The method also allows organizations to start with their existing workflow and drive evolutionary change. They can do this by visualizing their flow of work and further, limiting work in progress (WIP).[30] It is a simple process which gives you a visual aid to trigger only the requirements that you carry in your warehouse to serve each order you get from your customer. On the shop floor, it is a *Kanban* card to request an item from inventory while in the software world, it is the *Kanban* board. Sounds confusing? I'll give you a story.

This anecdote was told to me by an operations leader who had seen and transformed teams through Lean for twenty years. It was the early 1990s, and this professional worked for a huge manufacturing company in electronics business. He worked with a Japanese teacher (called *Sensei*, just like the ones in *The Karate Kid*).[31] His *Sensei* was responsible for leading the team from the front and ensuring that they had proper resources to work and learned all of the Japanese practices before he left them. While working with the Japanese used to be hard, as they were strict, it was really easy for him to gel with his *Sensei*, and they used to go out for dinners every now and then.

---

30. "Kanban," Agile Alliance, accessed September 9, 2020.
31. *The Trailer Guy*, "The Karate Kid (1984)—Movie Trailer," October 10, 2010, video, 2:11.

In a similar routine, the group went to a local multi-cuisine restaurant serving Japanese food. Sometimes, there were operators in the team who didn't know the Japanese teacher very well. They had some tough times with the teacher since they didn't like sudden changes in their work and used to mock the *Sensei* at times. While at the restaurant, they decided to prank him and one tried to mock his accent by asking the *Sensei* a question: "I still don't understand a *Kanban*—what is the deal with the *Kanban?* Is it necessary?"

The *Sensei* smiled and took the opportunity to show the magic. He took his beer bottle, drank it all, and laid it down on the table, sideways. Empty, obviously. Then he called the waitress over, who was Japanese, and started giving the dinner order to her in Japanese. He drew everyone's attention to where he was pointing at that bottle. The waitress looked at the bottle lying sideways, took it off, came back with another full bottle, then went away swiftly. People who understood this activity started smiling, but there was a final lesson that *Sensei* still had to deliver. The *Sensei* spoke to everyone, "The empty bottle laying like that is a signal to her to bring me another one." The operators started grinning and the whole table started doing the same thing. Once they did the sideways bottle act and took a few of those Japanese Sake beers from that dinner, they had loosened up with the *Sensei* and also learnt an interesting lesson on the importance of *Kanban* in their own work.

In the manufacturing space, we use cards to signal the warehouse or the supplier to send more material for a particular product to be made. Ideally, this creates a "pull" in the system and there is no need to store extra parts. But, in reality, we still use a huge amount of data to optimize our inventory operations. It is hard to reach a zero level of inventory because of constant demand fluctuations. More about that later.

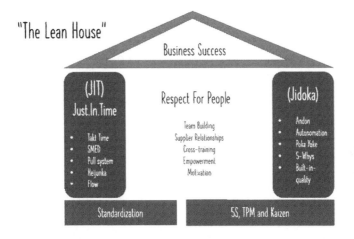

Figure 1: A description of basic Lean tools and how they are structured under the two pillars of JIT and *Jidoka*.

Muda

Muda is a Japanese word for "waste."[32] No one likes to pay for wasteful activities. Hence, this word is an "enemy" of operational excellence. Unfortunately, you may never be able to remove *Muda* from your work completely! In fact, just like the good cholesterol and bad cholesterol in your body, there is good or "essential" *Muda* and bad or "non-essential" *Muda*.

---

32. Doanh Do, "What is Muda, Mura, and Muri?" The Lean Way, August 5, 2017.

During my last year of MBA, I was attending my supply chain management class sitting next to a former marketing professional. He was one of my friends and someone who promised to help me with my global marketing midterms if I helped him understand the concepts of operations better. The class, as usual, was having an in-depth discussion on supply chain principles when the professor uttered "TIM-WOOD" in the middle of his class.[33] Now, as students of supply chain who had already gone through a basic operations class before, he was expecting us to understand what he meant. This somehow went unquestioned as the professor paced through the class to cover his time.

After the class was over, my friend approached me, sitting on one of the brown leather sofas on the second floor of our MBA building, and casually asked me, "What is TIM-WOOD?" What our professor had used is an acronym for the seven types of waste in a process. Now, my trainers have taught me that you can find them in any process happening around you. You just need a "Lean eye" to spot them. I saw this as an opportunity to explain him the concepts of *Muda* through his own eyes. I took him to our program's career center, which was located across the hall from our seats and was sure that I'd find at least five, if not all seven, of "TIMWOOD."

The moment we entered the career center, I spotted the receptionist arranging some files in a cabinet in front of her desk. I asked my friend to act like we were waiting for someone there and notice the way she was doing her file arrangement. She was stepping away from cabinet and taking one file at a time from the table. That was an easy one. I told

---

33. Nawras Skhmot, "The 8 Wastes of Lean," The Lean Way, August 5, 2017.

him that was the first one: transportation. Every time she takes steps to reach the file, she is travelling multiple times unnecessarily. Then I indicated to my friend about how she was not doing a one-time pick and drop. She was trying to set the files upright by fiddling with each of them multiple times. It is also an example of "over processing" since she doesn't need to be that meticulous, as no one is benefiting from her arrangement of files at a particular angle.

Next is I, which stands for "inventory." I pointed to the number of pages on her desk, which were supposedly pending for approvals and signoffs. I could have also shown my friend the list of unopened emails on her screen if I had access. In office work, not being able to open emails is the biggest information inventory waste that we have.

Next is M and W. They stand for "motion" and "waiting." I was among the four people waiting in the area that the receptionist had noticed but chose to put on standby until after her ordeal with the files ended. As a customer, waiting is totally prohibited in the Japanese Lean way of working. You are stalled if you wait for your next task and your efficiency drops. Also, you don't want your customers to wait for an output. Yet that was happening, and I could show it to my friend.

Next are the two Os. One stands for "overproduction" and the other for "over-processing." While I mentioned over-processing through the way she was spending time arranging the files at an angle, which was not needed, she had already committed the waste-crime of overproduction by calling more people than she could handle at one time. She was making the people wait in the area that had exceeded its capacity already and, well, she would be doing a lot more motion and transportation in bringing everyone to the right career coach every few minutes. Nothing against her, though.

The last one is D, which stands for "defects." Well, the receptionist was perfect enough to not show any symptoms of a defect in her work but by that time, my friend understood the whole story and was smart enough to get what defect would mean in terms of a process waste. After all, no one wants a defective product. Right?

Jidoka

Jidoka stands for automation with a human touch. Any machine that is expected to be controlled by human, needs to have an indication or a feedback system to signal the team of important issues. *Jidoka* is one of the two main pillars of Lean, the other one being JIT.[34] If you are working on an assembly line and make a mistake, you should be able to signal the team that you just made one. That's called *Andon*—a system where you push a button or pull a rope to announce that there is an issue worth looking at. For *Jidoka*, it is very important to have an automatic stop for any kind of abnormality, from quality problems to machine issues to running out of material. If the machine would continue with this abnormality, the costs would multiply down the line. So, the automation part is the system which generates the alarm. A more essential part of *Jidoka* is the human touch. It is the operator whose cognitive ability is responsible for generating

---

34. Christopher Roser, "What Exactly is Jidoka?" All About Lean, July 17, 2018.

that alarm. The operator is the one to spot the problem, stop the line, and fix it for everyone.

In factories, if the operators are working with a drilling machine, they have to set their metal piece and push two buttons simultaneously, one by each hand. This ensures that their hands are safe while starting the machine. This kind of a system makes safety a foolproof measure. In Japanese terms, it is called *Poka-Yoke*. Both *Andon* and *Poka-Yoke* are two of the many elements used to make the workplace safer, visually controlled, and automated with human touch.

Value Stream Mapping

Value stream mapping is a Lean tool which helps visualizing the flow of material and information (A "map" that displays a "stream" of "value-addition"). It is a visual tool that displays all critical steps in a specific process and quantifies the time and volume taken at each stage. It is basically a kind of GPS that helps every operations team in a company to locate where they are adding "value" to their product right from supplier end to customer services.

Imagine creating a sequence of processes starting from raw material that is transported to the production plant, stays there in the warehouse, then is transported to the line, assembled on the product, sent to the finished warehouse, serviced for the customer, sent to the point of sale, and then acquired by customer. This simple chain is an example of value addition from raw material version to the finished product. Complexity comes when you include different geographies, multiple parts, and more stages of production. A value stream map and the pull system are the two most important things you need to implement as soon as you can. There's generally a lot of pushback because it changes the way a team functions, causing the push system. But the impact is huge. A lot of people ignore the fact that value stream mapping is incredibly valuable, and everything needs to be designed around that pull system.

Value stream mapping helped me to get a thirty-thousand-foot view of where I was and what critical path meant to me and my work. As a new manager on the assembly line, it is not the culture that makes you stressed. It's the detail of the value stream. Because you are in a critical path of the process, you are not expected to fail. And everyone understands that. You do whatever it takes to get your critical path elements lined up and running daily.

CHAPTER 3

SOFTWARE IS EATING THE WORLD

———

The year 2007 brought a lot of surprises for me. For those of you who know about flip phones, the Moto Razr from Motorola used to be one of the coolest gadgets out there (I was psyched that they relaunched it in November 2019 with a foldable touchscreen).[35] But 2007 was different and a milestone in the journey of digital technology in a lot of ways. Personally, amidst the chaotic high school life that I was going through that year, I became a lot more curious about technology around me. The first thing that caught my attention was the news of the iPhone from Apple.[36] The company launched a phone with a completely flat screen, without buttons, and a cool, sleek look, which was a new experience. I was amazed but a bit worried by its design.

---

35. Sascha Segan, "A Visual History of the Motorola Razr," *PCMag*, November 13, 2019.
36. April Montgomery and Ken Mingis, "The Evolution of Apple's iPhone," *Computerworld*, October 15, 2020.

My mind immediately went toward the screen, its structure, and its build. I thought, "Well, it is one innocent drop away from breaking its screen and ruining the phone. Touchscreen would never work." But today, I don't think there is anyone, even in India, who uses a "candy bar" (yes, that's the official name for your beloved phones with a keypad and a small screen) or a flip phone with buttons. This was a digital change that intrigues me even now. How did we get to a point of staring at huge six-inch screens from using phones for a simple call in a matter of a decade?

Another major breakthrough for the Indian market that year was the launch of the company Flipkart, a formidable India-born rival to Amazon. That year marked the beginning of e-commerce revolution in India. It was around this same time that the Chinese online eCommerce counterpart Alibaba went public in the Hong Kong stock exchange.[37] The sudden rise of such solutions increased the importance of the digital world in my life. As an ardent shopper, I found myself spending more time on my laptop than on TV or visiting a physical store. The same shift happened with my viewership of advertisements too. Since I was spending more screen time on Facebook and YouTube, brands followed me with their advertisements.

There was a gradual change in my social behavior too. I switched from calling my friends to wish them birthdays to texting them or tagging them to posts on Facebook. Doesn't it remind you of the Netflix show *The Social Dilemma*?[38] This is a documentary on the impact of social media on our lives, and it is worth watching if you haven't seen it yet. When

---

37. Tony Munroe, "Alibaba.com Shares Soar in Trading Debut," *Reuters*, November 5, 2007.

38. "The Social Dilemma," Netflix, January 26,2019, video, 1:34:36.

you think about the engineers behind this transformation of social dynamics and shopping styles—or rather, lifestyles—they would have worked hours in front of their screens trying to master the best coding for these seamless services for the customers like me. All of it is digital. All of it is in front of you, distracting the consumer mind to click content online and pay for the products.

Aren't we cruising in the same mode even now? According to a recent research report from IDC (International Data Corp), almost 80 percent of smartphone users check their phones within fifteen minutes of waking up in the morning.[39] It is scary to see the community response to software solutions over the last ten years. We have shrunk our interaction space to a phone and a laptop. Even as I'm writing these words, it is 6:30 pm, and I should be outside having a walk or a casual meetup or chit-chat, but I have multiple reasons to stay indoors now. Thanks, pandemic. Although software has eaten all our daily tasks from waking up, working, travelling, and eating, I'll focus on an interesting case study about America's favorite food, pizza, from Domino's.

Getting food for ourselves and our families has been one of the most pristine activities. Hunters and gatherers did that on their own, and farmers have seen tons of changes in the way they grow crops and breed animals for meat. Domino's embodies a simple chain where software influenced so much of their operations that it is swiftly moving toward the future of how we get meals on our plates. To get a Domino's pizza at your place within thirty minutes, each step in the operation evolves until the pizza is delivered. At least, that

---

39. Jari Roomer, "3 Reasons Why You Shouldn't Check Your Phone Within 1 Hour of Waking Up," *Medium* (Blog), July 31, 2019.

is the utopian vision for Lean process practitioners working on that operation as they would call it *Kaizen*, or continuous improvement. Creating a pizza is an end-to-end procedure of value additions from multiple points which companies want to make cost-effective, flexible, attractive, and high-quality all at the same time.

Domino's and the Cloud Kitchen Concept

Domino's remained afloat during the 2020 pandemic as it already adopted "cloud kitchens" before this became standard.[40] Cloud kitchen is a concept popularized after ex-CEO of Uber, Travis Kalanick, pursued this idea.[41] Cloud kitchen is a concept devoted completely to online orders. The setup is made for online delivery of food as a norm, completely removing the need for dining halls or waiters. Travis believes there is no point in maintaining a real estate and extra staff to serve customers if the company can make money with food delivery over an app.[42] For over a decade, Domino's has been reaping benefits of a strategy involving optimizing store spaces for delivery, real estate locations with best routes in mind, and a high turnover for inventory in each store. Food delivery has high fixed costs. The courier requires a minimum wage. The ingredients can only be so cheap. There just aren't a ton of things throughout the food delivery value

40. Adam Keesling, "How Domino's Won the Pandemic," *Marker* (blog), May 24, 2020.
41. Naveen Sharda, "Serving Food from the Cloud," Toptal, accessed October 29, 2020.
42. Katie Canales, "Ousted Uber cofounder Travis Kalanick has reportedly spent $130 million on his ghost kitchen startup. Here's what it's like inside one of the secretive locations," *Businessinsider,* October 20, 2020.

chain that restaurants can innovate on without significant technological advances.

Domino's has actively strived to be ahead of its time by thinking about these constraints. It has had the foresight to optimize resources for delivery, place stores in low-cost and route-optimized retail locations, and build a digital presence through an app that really works, all of which is now paying off.

The journey of an order at Domino's can take us through the biggest transformations that software has done there. The moment you get lured with those new pizza toppings or that coupon you got from Domino's and decided to order, you are directed toward the Domino's website. Fun fact: the first coupon promos were started in 1957 by the Nielsen Coupon Clearing House. Domino's picked up on that trend after it got established in 1960 and used it as one of its marketing tricks from the very start.[43] Like every other retailer now, Domino's maintains a good history of your previous orders and helps you curate your order. It is received by the operations team of the closest delivery center located on a highway.

Dominos is smart in its operating style. It cares about its metrics. The first thing that the team targets is shorter production cycles. A manufacturing software could quicken the order processing by planning the orders in a sequence and ovens which can be timed to set their temperatures according to the type of pizza in it. By knowing which pizza takes a longer time, the sequences can be improved. In reality, this is what ERP systems (Enterprise Resource Planning) do for the businesses. They allow teams to track and streamline the order journey from origination to the completion of the

---

43. Jean Chatzky, "A Non-Boring History of Coupons," Retailmenot, September 1, 2015.

shipment. This is achieved via statistical snapshots of the warehouse and factory routines. The software enables an increased visibility, transparency, and control of the process, which, in our case, is procuring the raw veggies and protein and making the choice of dough.[44]

The next metric they focus on is lead time. It's common for manufacturing processes to be disrupted because different materials arrive at different times. No more than ten years ago, I never saw any trucks with GPS or a tracking iPad in the fleet manager's hand to track different metrics. Now every crucial stage in a supply chain, from supplier dispatch to customer delivery, is interlinked and laced with data points to provide a streamlined tracking. For Domino's, some inventory items are delivered daily, such as dough and sauce pre-mix, and the inventory management becomes just-in-time. Buffer stock of frozen ingredients is kept on hand. There have been plans to use technology for ordering, delivery, and purchasing process like mobile ordering, pizza tracker, PULSE data management system, DRU ("Domino's Robotic Unit"), and drone tech.[45]

All of these technologies support in-time delivery of products at the right outlet when required. They might experience weekly production delays because they're waiting for essential deliveries. For all the stores in the US and around the globe, various ingredients are sourced from different regions. The deli meats are sourced from Tibaldi in Melbourne, other ingredients come from Comgroup in Brisbane, and cheese and cheese blends are sourced from Leprino Foods in the

---

44. "Manufacturing Process Software: How It Works," Selecthub, accessed October 29, 2020.

45. Ibid.

US.[46] While manufacturing process software would not force all of these locations to go faster during a delay, it does make it easier to track the status of key parts and components.

Your order is prepared with a quality standard in mind. Nothing would be worse for Domino's than to see a perfectly timed delivery with a box of pizza without any toppings. Creates a crazy scene, doesn't it? Automation is the key to greater productivity for manufacturing businesses. Every component of the order is constructed in conjunction with an optimized "build plan" or standard operating procedure. You'll see fewer mistakes and find it easier to hit the targets (also known as company key performance indicators, or KPIs) if each operation is directed by a series of demonstrable digital commands. For Domino's, these KPIs are not just limited to tasty food, but also include friendly and helpful interactions with staff, clean stores, courteous delivery drivers, a website that is easy to navigate, and online ordering that operates without malfunctions.

At this point, with the right ingredients sourced globally and the help of their order sequencing programs, the order is prepared and relayed to you through a message and an email in your inbox. Quality is also determined by the consistency of outputs. This means they don't want it to be 100 percent always. They can live with 90 percent if it stays that way for every incoming order for the team. Data is used to increase information flow in the team.[47] In addition to the production staff, customers also benefit from greater visibility and the power to track their order. This information is also passed on to sales and marketing departments, where it is used to

---

46. "Dominos Operations," Infographic, Coggle, accessed October 29, 2020.
47. Ibid.

build up complete product histories. They can use the data to keep them informed about their orders. Visibility is a top priority for consumers, so being able to do this is a way to increase customer satisfaction.

Now the point comes in your order when a delivery comes at your doorstep with the pizza. When software solutions are skillfully employed, they also share the geo-location and most optimal routes (which is now carried by one solution: Google Maps). These software also initially help in telling the most optimal location while setting up a store and store layouts. This is very important, as manufacturers can alter material movements within the store by changing their pathways. That is why you seldom find a Domino's store embedded in a mall, but find more stories right outside on a highway. This is for a simple reason: to make deliveries faster.

"Voice of customer" is a term used for customer feedback.[48] Keeping up with current times, Domino's sources all this feedback through marketing tie-ups with food websites and apps, which ask for your rating and put in a Google review. Dominos would use it as a feedback loop to analyze each evening, week, and month to improve.

Domino's proved to the world that taking a step in advance to improve on technology can help you prepare for future customers better. It would not be easy to introduce the online ordering option in 2005, when people were still enjoying their rooftop dinners in-person all over the world. It would also be hard for the Domino's team to put trust in an iPhone app to order food online in 2009, when their closest competitors were not doing the same. DRUs and drones are

---

48. "What is Voice of the Customer (VoC)?" Qualtrics, accessed October 29, 2020.

some of their future innovations to reduce cooking times to three minutes in-store and delivery times to ten minutes.[49]

At present, the food industry is constrained by multiple things. Uber Eats, DoorDash, and Grubhub were the result of eaters feeling lazy and not wanting to come out and eat.[50] So were the wave of different meal kit delivery solutions like HelloFresh, Home Chef and Blue Apron.[51] Software influence started from giving an outlet to consumers on the internet but has grown to being available a few clicks away on our phone. I remember taking out time every Sunday for getting groceries for home, but now I order on Walmart or Instacart. There are so many solutions available just to cover the distance between my room and my kitchen stove, that I don't even have to get up from the couch to do anything. The last two things remaining are maybe putting the food from my plate into my mouth and digesting it. I hope there is no app created for those things!

This example is just one among the thousands that shows digital is the way of life. If we really want to view the processes and take a leaf out of the Domino's story, it should be the one where they are open to evolution, changing systems, and *Kaizen.* For any industry, it matters when they realize the space around them is changing, and they anticipate their customers' preferences in not only *what* they want but *how* they want it.

49. "Dominos Operations," Infographic, Coggle, accessed October 29, 2020.
50. Sunny Dhillon, Kevin Wu, "Delivery 2.0: How on-demand meal services will become something far bigger," Fast Company, February 15, 2021.
51. David Weliver, "Meal Delivery Comparison: Home Chef vs. HelloFresh vs. Blue Apron vs. Freshly vs. EveryPlate vs. Sunbasket," *Money Under 30,* last modified: February 7, 2021.

CHAPTER 4

CASE 1 | AUTO INDUSTRY EXPLORATION—WHERE IT ALL STARTED

———

Human beings are artists; we are not manufacturers.
We are not accurate or precise—both of which we want
in manufacturing.

—UNKNOWN

Automotive Industry—Where It All started

The best thing that happened to me was meeting over five hundred people in my couple years of work. You can meet or befriend that many people online, but can you really do it in person? Well, if you're in a factory with over seven thousand people, five hundred is still a small percentage. This is a story of how I started opening up to a new world of practical knowledge that came from a simple, innocent training. I came closer to those experiences as I met those experiences again and again over the last ten years.

My favorite class at Delhi College of Engineering was operations research. The college had very few star professors and most of them belonged to our department. All of them had one thing in common: passion for their subject. It made the students interested and passionate for their classes. Operations research, as one of my seniors had mentioned, is an evergreen concept. I had been hooked on this word—*evergreen*. When I considered pursuing engineering, I had overheard a conversation between a group of parents exclaiming, "Computers are the latest thing but let me tell you, mechanical and civil engineering departments can never go out of business—they are *evergreen*." I followed those footsteps, and something told me operations research had a similar magic.

My first OR (operations research) class was the most challenging one. It felt as if I had jumped on a moving train without realizing where the train was going. But one concept saved my life: MOST. This stands for Maynard Operation Sequence Technique and is one of the gold standards in measuring work motions. It basically involves both time study and work study concepts. Every step to do a particular task is analyzed: the operator switching on a piece of equipment, lifting the tool, using the tool, placing the tool back at its location, etc. MOST analysis is a complete study of an operation or sub-operation typically consisting of several method steps and a corresponding sequence model. The smallest unit is called a TMU, which is equivalent to 1/28th of a second, or 0.0036 seconds.[52] You can challenge Neo from *The Matrix* to

---

52. *Anant Awasare*, "How to calculate standard time by using MOST Maynard Operation Sequence Technique," May 31, 2018, video, 6:24.

capture that kind of action.[53]

I never got to break any process down to that level, but it feels fascinating to just know that such level exists. Consider a simple work of picking up a glass of water. Now, imagine breaking apart all the movements you did in this process through TMUs to the fifth decimal place of a second. Yes, I'm talking about even a single movement of muscle—it gets counted here. But MOST also helps in describing the way the hand approaches, how the tool is held, and which direction it is picked up. The business of measuring a work motion is many times more complicated. While learning it the first time, I would have shrugged and laughed if someone told me that people have spent lives studying this one concept. But it is, indeed, fascinating.

In 2012, Yamaha Motor, situated in the outskirts of Greater Noida in Northern India, became my first play-ground or rather, battlefield of sorts, to test what I learnt in my industrial engineering class.[54] I was right in the middle of one of the most intense processes in automotive industry… frame welding shop. This single shop generated structural frames of sports bikes like the legendary RX100. This bike has a legacy in India and has been a heartthrob for Indian bikers since the 1980s but was restricted to only export in South Asia in 2012. I also saw the R15 (the highest-end sports bike boasting a 0 to 60 km per hour in 5 seconds).[55] I stood in front of a giant workshop which said "Body in White" outside. That first smell of fumes of MIG welding that I got was so peculiar, and by then I had made up my mind that

53. *Flashback FM*, "Neo—'The One' | The Matrix [Open Matte]", November 11, 2016, video, 3:58.
54. "Products—Yamaha,", Yamaha Motors India, accessed August 1, 2020.
55. Ibid.

this would be my home for the next three months. I had the utmost joy of an auto enthusiast upon entering a facility like this, but soon, I would be wound up with rules.

Among the first few rules that my manager explained about the facility, he explicitly said, "Do not wander outside this shop more than once a day when you go for lunch!" So, he basically meant that I would be locked in this smoke-bil-lowing-ever-scary-monstrous-machines-bound welding shop when all I could think about was how many pictures I could have taken of those sports bikes getting assembled next door. An urge grows more when someone forbids you from it. It is like the forbidden apple. I wanted to soak up all the good smells of the new bikes in the outbound lot whenever I got a chance.

Apart from that fanboy moment, every day I noticed all the Japanese principles of 5S and *Kaizen* that I had learned being followed religiously there. I was lucky to be learning it, firsthand, from a Japanese company. 5S is a concept that teaches hygiene and promotes the use of discipline and order-liness in your workplace. Remember Marie Kondo and her positive energy ringing from items that you possess? She also teaches this concept of 5S.[56] My first job was to identify all cases on the shop floor that violated these five principles, from the start of the shift to the finish.

My trainer was an Indian guy with a thick Bangla accent. I was fascinated by the way he remembered all the Japanese terms and repeated them every single time to feed them to our minds. "*Seiri, Seiso, Seiton, Seiketsu, Shitsuke... Seiri, Seiso, Seiton, Seiketsu, Shitsuke...*" His method worked, as I

---

56. Adam Henshell, "Improve Organization with 5S: The Theory Behind Marie Kondo," *Process Street* (blog), March 15, 2019.

still remember these five words as they resonate in my mind in his peculiar accent. These, as we saw in the earlier chapter, mean sorting, cleanliness, orderliness, standardization, and sustain, in that order.

Kaizen means continuous improvement. That was my primary work after conducting my MOST studies. As a part of a team, I got to know about a traditional type of welding called MIG welding and a new technique to provide protective layer to bike exhausts called shot blasting techniques from the experts who had worked there for over fifteen years. I stood on the shop floor with a stopwatch in my hand, watching every movement, and sometimes making handwritten notes of the movements, as videotaping was not allowed on the shopfloor. It was not mere note-taking. The hardest part was standing for over six hours on the floor every day, shadowing an annoyed operator and expecting that he would repeat his steps at least three times for me to have a valid process record. At the end of the day, I would generally finish up with over twenty-five written pages of notes for about ten or eleven processes and time readings for each of them. Then, the process of *Kaizen* would start.

The manager had a really good eye for all the processes. He used to close his eyes and sit in front of his desk, asking me to narrate the process step-by-step. His experience on the shop floor allowed him to fill all the gaps in my process description and tell me which steps seemed odd or required a *Kaizen*. I wouldn't be surprised with him taking the precise name of the person working on the process and his shift to tell me whom to contact for the *Kaizen* event. He practically *lived* there and knew the whole shop. These first few months were really dynamic, and I came out with a report on five process improvements in my short span of three months.

This first introduction of Lean manufacturing was important to me. When I look back at this experience, I get frustrated at my manager for keeping me busy with this mundane work because it was part of a much bigger organizational culture problem that he never shared with me. At that time, I had no clue that anything requiring people to change the way they work drives them away from those initiatives. Even many from the senior leadership didn't care about this fact. But it gave me a very critical on-the-ground experience of the extent of effort required to correct one process. I was also mentally ready to take on any kind of on-field project after this internship, which, two years later, would be waiting for me at Tata.

It was October 2013 when, during an on-campus placement drive, the day of my selection at Tata Motors finally came. After a grueling written round, group discussion, and two rounds of personal interviews, I was among the seven to-be engineers, selected as graduate engineering trainees at Tata. For GETs, or the "Graduate Engineering Trainees," the first few weeks consist of long training and introductions to the company. Since there is no particular department or a single boss that a GET reports to, they are given an opportunity to explore any part of the office and talk to all the seniors as they like. However, this extent of freedom varies with companies. The only next time you get a similar feeling of freedom is when you give a month's notice before leaving the company. So, it is kind of precious. I would guess that feeling is common to everyone, irrespective of whether you are a GET or not. In my "exploration period," apart from hanging around in the canteen and HR's conference rooms, I also got a craving to visit the shopfloor and view those behemoth trucks being produced one after the other. I quickly realized that my knowledge of Lean had some real scope of work there. That thought turned into excitement when I heard a manager talking about some Japanese folks coming to the plant to start a project on Lean.

Figure 2: Tata Motors, Pune plant

After that magical period was over, I was back to the muggle world ready to deal with real problems. Every trainee was assigned to a department based on how the GETs performed during the training and a series of tests, and then a priority list was made for each one. I was assigned manufacturing, and that's what I secretly wanted, although everyone aspired to join the research and development team. More specifically, I was assigned the assembly shop, and I was elated to join.

"No more welding," I thought. But the assembly line is a different level of complexity. It is where over two thousand parts come together to give shape to the final vehicle. That means two thousand different ways to screw up a fully functioning vehicle if you are not careful about quality. It also means two thousand opportunities to learn and relearn about how the product functions. My manager quickly identified my inclination toward Lean and work study, and I was sent to join that coveted Japanese training for Lean manufacturing.

"But I am already trained in the Lean processes from my work at Yamaha!" I notified my manager, to which he said, "This is Tata, and there are many things different from a bike company that you have learnt before. *Enjoy kar yaar!*"

The last sentence means, enjoy your time there! Well, for me, it was another month of arduous training, wandering around conference rooms, and mugging up the same stuff I knew from before. Lean principles don't change. It is the different problems that you tackle with the same tools that increases your learning. After the training, I had an itch to implement things and solve problems. Although most of the things in my training remained similar to what I learnt at Yamaha, I learned new processes called standardized work and the team leader concept. Around the same time, there was another project on supplier relationship transformation. Both of these were part of a transformation journey which required total change of mindset and also required us to use scientific tools for problem solving.

In all of our production plants, we took model lines and model suppliers and trained around two hundred people under the guidance of Professor Shoji Shiba and Mr. Takeyuki Furuhashi. Over the course of nine months, we were able to get substantial success both in our plants and at our suppliers' end. Tata Motors has grown manifolds in the past couple of decades. While I had seen established production processes, there was a need to standardize the basic processes across all plants. This would help to smoothly cater to the market from various manufacturing locations across India. We were able to achieve just that with the Lean tools for production planning, scheduling, requesting materials from external suppliers, and assignment of manpower based on activities. It is a completely integrated approach impacting all areas of manufacturing.

There are several challenges in the process—creating a store for finished goods, generating an assembly sequence list, and making common trolleys, to name a few. Generating sequence can encompass anything from a simple bolt and nut rolled clockwise, involving five steps, to a complex engine being aligned with rest of the vehicle body by four operators at once. Before this concept, many such improvements would fall under different functions; Thus, the improvements were not aligned to a common objective. Often, improvements in one area could become an impediment to another.

Tata and Beyond

The standardized work as a practice is not limited to rearranging these trolleys and generating assembly sequence. In general, it takes a lot of initiative from the manager's side to maintain a hierarchy in the organization and keep implementing an updated process, keeping the critical communication between the supervisor and senior manager intact. When you combine the whole chain of information, it becomes overwhelming to keep up with standard work process. I dealt with almost twenty-five to thirty new updates every day due to some new safety points, a new tool introduced, or a common trolley deployed that changed the process drastically. Communicating this change meant that I would send an update to my divisional manager and also go on the assembly line and train the supervisor for its implementation, all in the same day.

Everything that I learned was mostly manual at Tata, although, unlike Yamaha, I was at a liberty to video record my observations and come back with more accurate measurements and improvements of processes observed. After almost six years of that project, I have seen a drastic change in the level of automation involved in the building of the same trucks and a dependence on a network of sensors that keep the vehicles safe and functional. To gather more insights on how those processes differ for electric vehicles, I ventured into a fantastic start-up called Canoo, which is partnering with Hyundai to develop an autonomous electric SUV. The concept comes as a part of almost twenty-one other companies that are operational in Silicon Valley, as of 2020, developing their versions of future mobility solutions. Traditional auto giants including Volkswagen, Ford, and General Motors are at the forefront supporting many of these start-ups.[57]

I met with Rishav from Canoo to understand how operations differed for him. Rishav is an on-ground operations specialist and helped the company with production and field simulations of the product. He had previously worked for another start-up called Faraday Future, working on electric

57. Sean O'Kane, "Hyundai will build electric vehicles with EV startup Canoo," *The Verge*, February 11, 2020.

vehicles.[58] He told me, "If you think about what these companies are trying to do, they are start-ups with no organizational history. They have no methodologies, they have no principles, they have no battle scars. At Faraday, we just solved that problem by throwing bodies at it. We just had an abundance of talent. And then as we got organized and adopted Lean methodologies by working through Six Sigma and DMAIC and *Kaizen*."

And he is right! Start-ups are too primitive to think about optimization in their initial growth phase. They are burning money perfecting the product and doing a lot of marketing. They are pursuing a viable product and need to experiment, learn, and relearn before thinking about frugality and optimization. If you don't do that, you're basically putting the cart before the horse. You're going to spend more money some other day, rather than doing it now. People just start without having the experience and then decide to figure it out later. However, even at this stage, evaluating Lean doesn't hurt anyone.

The discussion about an electric vehicle wouldn't be complete without mentioning the company of the century, Tesla.[59] This company has proven that with a revolutionary product, one doesn't have to wait a century to achieve a fifty-billion-dollar valuation. Derek is a Lean expert from Tesla who helped me get a better idea of the company's philosophy. "Lean at Tesla was more used as a set of principles to identify and remove waste from the system, including line balancing, standardization, immediate reaction to quality abnormalities,

---

58. "Experience a New Species—Faraday Future," Faraday Future, accessed August 1, 2020.

59. Graham Immerman, "Elon Musk Focusing on Tesla Lean Manufacturing," Machine Metrics, February 20, 2018.

and error proofing." The launch of the mass market Tesla Model 3 has been dogged by production problems with the number of unfulfilled orders exceeding the ability of the company to deliver. Tesla CEO Elon Musk has talked about being in a "production hell"—working tirelessly to get production moving at the right pace. But they are determined to make the processes as efficient as possible.[60]

Did you know Elon Musk hates the conveyors at the Tesla production plants? He says, "The biggest mistake we made was trying to automate general assembly, where everything is put together." The removal of conveyors—which Musk said ended up complicating things even more—is another indication that Lean manufacturing principles are at root at Tesla. Conveyors added a level of complexity that led to lower productivity. The conveyors needed constant attention from engineers so that they did not break down. Removing things that do not add value is a major activity when doing Lean manufacturing.[61]

Rishav now works in a different company called Blue Robotics. It exclusively deals with underwater autonomous vehicles submersible up to nine hundred meters of depth.[62] He leads manufacturing there. He remarks, "Before starting at the company, I had a meeting with the CEO, the director of manufacturing, and the director of sales and marketing and I told them, 'Hey guys, we are going to slow down the line.' Now we are month and a half into building the line and it is running slower. Pandemic downtime has helped us and actually evened everything out for us." One needs time

60. "The Lean Transformation of Tesla and Elon Musk," Lean Factories, accessed August 5, 2020.

61. Ibid.

62. "Our Story," Blue Robotics, accessed August 5, 2020.

to set up processes, analyze them for effectiveness, and go back on the line for final delivery. It was interesting to learn that even for startups, the Lean process remains mostly same when only manufacturing is involved.

"Everybody's seen the light at the end of the tunnel. Previously, manufacturing was a black hole for them, but now we can totally see that, you know, we can totally get out of this black hole," Rishav added. Blue Robotics has started making revenue and is selling tens of thousands of their product. It seems one of the aspects of culture is that Lean doesn't make sense unless you are making revenue.

However, does this change with the inclusion of software in the company? For automobiles, there's an intersection between software and hardware, which is called a hardware test. Largely, the team which manages the testing and simulation has engineers who are the integrating touchpoints taking part with the manufacturing team in the product development meeting. When the mechanical guy says a mechanical number like torque, it has a different connotation and interpretation for an electrical guy. They understand current and an expert from software team will talk about codes and commands and sensor inputs. The hardware testing guy is the only person who actually understands how to interface all these things inside the machine. He is actually the only one physically tightening the bolts that are conducting the current through the system, so he really gets what is going on. Rishav says, "The team at Blue Robotics relies very heavily on their hardware database. Without that team, it is hard to imagine a structured flow of information among teams. I think the top three things that one should be doing for developing Lean products in the future: testing, testing, and testing."

Tesla does something similar too. Although it is hard to separate out the hardware testing people from traditional manufacturing specialists, Elon Musk stresses on the need to trust human's potential. After all, humans *are* underrated.

PART 2

CHAPTER 5

DIGITAL VS PHYSICAL | FROM DUEL TO DUALITY

———

In the coming years, mobile devices will become the gateway to the physical world. Everything around us will be "taggable," "scannable," or "reachable." The world around us will become the interface.

—JO CAUDRON, AUTHOR—*DIGITAL TRANSFORMATION*[63]

Digital progress has had different timelines for different industries, even when it is attacked by a situation like the COVID-19 pandemic. The most impactful change that has happened due to the pandemic is reachability and connectivity between colleagues. Although work from home seemed like a distant utopian vision some time ago, it suddenly became a stark reality. A company like Twitter enjoyed the

---

63. Jo Caudron and Dado Van Peteghem, *Digital Transformation: A Model to Master Digital Disruption* (Belgium: Duval Union Consulting, January 2014).

new way of working and found a good reason to make working from home a standard option forever for its employees.[64] For another set of organizations, though, it was more like a nightmare. Federal offices found themselves playing catch up to this new reality. In a conversation with several federal government officials both in India and the US, I could sense the level of upgrade their teams received after "WFH" became a norm due to COVID-19. Even for my dad, who heads the DMV offices for a region in India, it was an urgent action to extend employments of database assistants in his offices, and the DMV forms started getting filled online for the first time. He has a separate login to join meetings virtually from home, which is kind of cool.

This progress is not restricted to a certain type of industry. It varies with the countries, economic developments there, the maturity of an organization, and the target consumers that it serves. Banks in Asia have a very different timeline to implement digital processes than banks in the developed nations of the west. Asian customers in the villages and small cities are slower in transitioning to digital payments and payment wallets or making use of the credit/debit cards. They predominantly believe in keeping cash or saving through a "FD" or fixed deposit in the banks at most.[65] The general demography and income level in Asia is skewed toward majority middle-class people who still understand physical currency better than digital wallets. It is the decade of the 2020s, where digital wallets are on the rise and are completely changing the scene of banking in countries like India and

---

64. Elizabeth Dwoskin, "Americans might never come back to the office, and Twitter is leading the charge," *The Washington Post*, October 1, 2020.
65. Jacob Dahl, Ervin Ng and Joydeep Sengupta, "How Asia is reinventing banking for the digital age," McKinsey, February 11, 2020.

China.[66] Another example is manufacturing in China, which is profitable to the world because it can boast of its low-cost and highly flexible workforce. It doesn't pay to mechanize a company in China if the mechanization would cost you more in the long run. If the company is already operating in the cheapest way possible, mechanization and automation will only complicate things and raise costs. That's why manual workforce still holds effective there.

This disparity creates a need to consider different operational routes for product makers and software architects to achieve their end goals of a profitable product or service and a happy customer. The technological changes around the globe point toward some critical challenges that companies face today to improve their daily operations. There is a need to understand the influence of digital solutions on the end consumer. Take supply chain as an example. Most of the time, it is an amalgamation of data-driven decision-making and its eventual execution by physical movement of trucks. You cannot make an app to completely eliminate freight movement from the globe. But yes, you can make smarter decisions to make it faster and remove wasteful pieces from the value chain. Similarly, with financial institutions, you may end up eliminating the needs of physical banks at some point, but there are many intangible aspects that will keep human interaction intact. Gartner says that day is coming fast for at least 80 percent of financial institutions by the next decade.[67]

---

66. Ibid.
67. "Most banks will Be made irrelevant by 2030—Gartner," *Finextra*, October 29, 2018.

In 2019, when Amazon came up with one-day delivery, it posed a huge challenge to its competitors.[68] The news talked about the millions of products moved around the globe by Amazon. But how does it look for the operations professionals working in an Amazon warehouse? Think of how much you need to do for delivering a package from its seller to the customer in only one day. This means there are only twenty-four hours for a manager to receive and process an order from the customer, locate the right product SKU (stock keeping unit) in their warehouse or procure it from the seller, package it, transport it, and deliver to the customer's door. The team would have to upgrade every lever and tighten every link in their supply chain to digital to ensure efficiency. Amazon does a perfect job thinking one step ahead of their customers and investing in forecasting. Amazon hates to see customers waiting for their products to be delivered to them by sellers or facing a shortage of stock and then sending a message of delay to their customers. Thus, Amazon is slowly zooming in on creating a Lean machine of delivery. After all, the end objective of Lean is to identify and eliminate or change any part of a process that does not add value.[69]

Even though the speed of transition is slow, an excessive sale of smartphones in the past decade has transformed the developing nations into a future digital playground for all. Countries like India are zooming past Europe in terms of number of unicorn start-ups every year (a unicorn start-up is a company that exceeds valuation of $1 billion). While the decade of the 2000s was dedicated to developing solutions

68. Jackie Wattles, "Amazon starts one-day shipping for millions of products," *CNN Business*, June 3, 2019.
69. Katie Schoolov, "How Amazon gets Prime Day orders to your house in just one day," *CNBC*, July 13, 2019.

"online" and converting the most valuable tasks digital, the decade of the 2010s was focused on utilizing mobile phone and making it powerful enough that there remains a limited need to even open your laptops.[70] In July 2020, an additional 113,000 new apps were published on the Google App store. It is impossible to fathom the amount of digitization that will happen in the next decade, which might transform many activities that we currently do day-to-day.[71] The developed world is ready to see the next change happen—the rise of AI.

My first interaction with digital transformation happened during my third week of my MBA, back in 2018. This was the time when I met a lot of consultants from various walks of life and worked in various industries. The first interaction that I remember was from a person from the consulting firm Ernst & Young (EY). He was a senior consultant there and a specialist in supply chain management. He told me that in today's business, the supply chain managers don't ask you to improve any process—they want to improve the plan behind that process. Most plans that the clients follow are manual, and they face a huge challenge to digitally transform their manual plan.

He gave me one example from Kroger. It uses a lot of robotic equipment, which are both more advanced and simpler than the ones used by Amazon collaborating with Kiva, a robotic manufacturer, as its choice for warehouse automation.[72] He explained the comparison as that of Amazon

70. Jennifer Rudden, "Number of unicorns worldwide as of January 2020, by country," Statista, Feb 7, 2020.
71. Mansoor Iqbal, "App Download and Usage Statistics (2020)," Business of Apps, October 30, 2020.
72. David Edwards, "Amazon Now Has 200,000 Robots Working in its Warehouses," *Robotics & Automation News*, January 21, 2020.

using a bicycle when Kroger has actually started building a sports bike for their operations. What is it that Kroger is doing differently apart from just adding a robot? It is not their employees or manpower—they focus more on where they can replace that manpower with robots, efficiency of equipment, accuracy of their operations. That idea gave me the insight that digital transformation can happen anywhere. I have an experience of working in warehouses, and I could never imagine stowing and racking up and other simple movement of items done completely by robots without the touch of any hands.

Kroger has managed to align its physical processes with automation and the Internet of things (IoT) in such a way that upskills its employees instead of removing them from the system. They were able to build a completely refreshed view of the warehouse operations that could be controlled by the bots rolling on a grid on the ceiling, picking, and dropping items per the customer orders. All of this is controlled with an intelligent *Jidoka* and IoT software solutions integrating the physical packages with online orders. This was my first inspiration to understand digital transformation better. I describe more about my inspiration from Kroger, which out-and-out challenged Amazon's capabilities and the specific case of its operations in a chapter later.

One concept which connects physical and digital realms is digital twins. A digital twin is a simulation for the developing of a physical product and anticipating the issues it might encounter. Imagine you had a perfect digital copy of the physical world. This twin would enable you to collaborate virtually, intake sensor data and simulate conditions quickly, understand what-if scenarios clearly, predict results more accurately, and output instructions to manipulate the physical world.

Digital twins can simulate any aspect of a physical object or process. They can represent a new product's engineering drawings or represent all the subcomponents and corresponding lineage in the broader supply chain from the design table all the way to the consumer—the "as built" digital twin. They may also take an "as maintained" form, a physical representation of equipment on the production floor. The simulation captures how the equipment operates, how engineers maintain it, or even how the goods this equipment manufactures relates to customers.[73]

Autopilot cars use it nowadays. One of my close friends, who dwells in Washington, DC, is obsessed with autonomous vehicles. He has pursued his dreams in discovering everything electric and anything automatic. During my MBA, I used to engage with him many times on the topic of data simulation vs actual drive testing a vehicle to improve its capabilities. I support data simulations as they provide the car with much needed scenario tests quickly. If you actually drive the car, the same data points might take up much more of your time and efforts, not mentioning the danger involved, too. When I told him about this analogy, he added, "It is cool to take out insights from your data, but you never know if you're completely missing a data 'oil well' while working on a single point of data in front of you."

He's right in a way. In the automotive industry, there are design software like CATIA and SOLIDWORKS, which help design different parts and need to be updated when the team wants to do some cost savings. Coming from a physical realm of processes myself, I have seen many of such cost-reduction

---

73. Scott Buchholz, Bill Briggs, "Tech Trends—2020," Deloitte Insights, January 15, 2020.

product trials fail, which otherwise look promising theoretically or on the software drawings. It is important to respect the physical efforts that companies like Tesla and more recently, Cruise Automation (a company working on autonomous vehicles and supported by General Motors), are putting into their work. Generating and using actual data prevents them from needing to use any kind of digital twin or simulation of what they want the sensors to do in an actual road situation.

Digital twin capabilities began as a tool of choice in the engineer's toolbox because they can streamline the design process and eliminate many aspects of prototype testing. Using 3D simulations and human-computer interfaces such as augmented reality and virtual reality (AR/VR), engineers can determine a product's specifications, how it will be built and with what materials, and how the design measures against relevant policies, standards, and regulations.[74] It helps engineers identify potential manufacturability, quality, and durability issues—all before the designs are finalized. Thus, the traditional prototyping process accelerates, with products moving into production more efficiently and at a lower cost.[75]

In the digital space, we are creating these data "oil wells" (more commonly termed "data lakes" in tech jargon) more quickly than we can even fathom. Every minute, over three hundred hours of content are uploaded on YouTube and five billion hours of videos are watched every day. Google encounters forty thousand new queries every second.[76] This

74. International Data Corporation, "Worldwide spending on cognitive and artificial intelligence systems forecast to reach $77.6 billion in 2022, according to new IDC spending guide," September 19, 2018.

75. Scott Buchholz, Bill Briggs, "Tech Trends—2020," Deloitte Insights, January 15, 2020.

76. Meg Prater, "25 Google Search Statistics to Bookmark ASAP," *Hubspot* (blog), accessed Sep 12, 2020.

is another level of a data "oil well" creation, isn't it? This grounds my belief, to say the least, that operations need data to thrive better. For some companies, though, the decision is to invest in the infrastructure and save in the future. For others, it bodes well to wait and adopt the most suitable version of the digital solution before investing right away. It saves them the time and money to pivot later.

The future of digital operations is in rapid expansion. Companies have heaps of data and they want to get quick benefits from it the moment they find a pattern. Since the biggest players in the retail, e-commerce, and digital worlds operate across international domains, they need to keep a balance between the expansion and control between geographies and functions. In Part Three, I'll discuss about the further effects of data as oil and their importance for the tools effective right now, AI and ML. They play a huge role in defining not only the processes, but complete business frameworks in many industries. Let's see how Lean comes into the picture when software eats the world and digital comes knocking on the door of service industry.

CHAPTER 6

THE BEYOND | LEAN
FOR SERVICE INDUSTRY

Not all Lean manufacturing ideas translate from factory floor to office cubicle.[77]

Lean has traditionally not been used in the service industry. For more emerging economies like India and China, the economic transition has been from being an agriculture-centric to a service-centric nation. However, there are some industries like textile and electronics for which these countries have become a center of mass production, most of it manual. India and China never took the longer route of starting from an "Industrial Revolution" and going step-by-step to understand the fundamentals of manufacturing but instead leapt many years forward to match up with the world. India especially evolved and specialized in its IT sector and provides a huge section of business process outsourcing (BPO)

---

77. Julia Hanna, "Bringing 'Lean' Principles to Service Industries," Harvard Business School, October 22, 2007.

services to western brands, even today. But, with changing times, as demand rises, they need to optimize.[78]

Everything from an innocent game app to the aspirational Uber is a form of service. While the products coming out of a manufacturing process are tangible, the services are essentially invisible, yet directly impact a customer. Industries like banks, telecommunication, healthcare, tourism, defense, and software are good examples for service industry. The supportive functions such as HR, finance, and customer service are also part of service processes. There might be differences in the ways these industries operate. However, they all exist for one reason: profit. Profit that they can acquire by either providing a premium service and at the same time operate efficiently. In the current market, where the customer has a choice for everything, companies in an industry fight to get a share of their time, attention, and money.[79]

Sometimes, these companies have to think about an efficient way to operate and keep their costs low and to increase profit margins. That is when they require efficiency to be added to their work. *But how do they define efficiency?* Even when we talk about manufacturing organizations, there are a boatload of service functions: IT, HR, security, facilities providers, customer support, internal consultants, and corporate strategy teams. These functions need to have measurable metrics to improve on their processes, become faster and cost-effective, and help the company's bottom line. The operations excellence team in your organization is also a support function. It provides a *service* by optimizing the

---

78. Tarun Khanna, "China + India: The Power of Two," *Harvard Business Review,* December 2007.

79. John Hagel III, John Seely Brown and Lang Davison, "Why Do Companies Exist?," *Harvard Business Review,* February 25, 2009.

resources and rolling out cost reduction plans and productivity improvement projects. What targets can you give to such a team? How can a COO measure their performance and eventually improve it?

I tried to explore the answers in my interviews. COVID-19 times have given us all a special way to start our days. While researching, I started every day with a new conversation on my workdays. I connected with Savita Gupta, a dynamic professional from India involved in multiple procurement teams from Airtel, L&T, and Coca Cola. Savita has great experience in handling enterprise services. My conversation was mostly focused on her experience at Airtel, India's telecom giant. She described her work with customer support service as the most crucial interaction with their end consumer. There were so many complexities she faced on both the demand and supply sides. On one hand, going with the customer demand, she had to go extra lengths to support her internal and external customers while providing them with wireless service connections. On the other hand, she had to worry about procuring items from her suppliers, dealing with enterprise partnerships, and the irregularities in that supply.

She says, "My team creates a new connection in a new place for a new face every time. They may not come back to us months after that connection and expect us to perfectly perform all the time." Airtel faces a tough competition from three other giants in the same area. There are so many factors to conquer simultaneously: price points, service features, customer resolution capabilities, and metrics.[80] Customers worry more about the minimum recharge or the web service.

---

80. Bharat Babu, "Competitive Position Analysis of Airtel," *Medium* (Blog), November 7, 2020.

It is a lot different than manufacturing organizations, where most operational excellence initiatives are applied in the field of material movement.

Ms. Gupta's idea of services is very simple—they are low on physical work and bring in high profits. But there is a challenge that services bring: data points. There is especially a dearth in the data points that are useful for internal operations of an organization. She remarks, "Airtel is one of the most advanced providers of communication technology in India. It promptly strives to give all the 4G connections to the most remote areas and automated routers, but we hardly get similar upgrades for internal operations that quickly." Coming from an Indian multinational conglomerate myself, I can agree to that.

One of the terms I remember from my work is "First Shot Okay." It refers to the number of times a product was made without any defects on the very first try. Think of it as a defect-free car coming out of an assembly line. You switch on the ignition and roll it off the line for use. Many of my fellow manufacturing people would still see it as the utopian vision because, with what I have seen on the shop floor, that actually happens just 45 to 50 percent of the time. That percentage is in a highly controlled environment. There are so many moving parts and tests for a complex product like a car that you need some form of rework. Now, think of Airtel. If Ms. Gupta gets relaxed with a 50 percent success, she might be busy with her team, just pacifying all the angry customers and justifying cancelled subscriptions. In the service industry, every time you open a new account, both you and the customer anticipate a service delivered first time right.

When you combine those two factors, you have a service industry reeling with low margins and high stress on cost control. Then smiling to their customers after all of this to make a good first impression. Ms. Gupta continues, "We do try to do both these things, but by deploying low-cost manpower and still going in a manual way, rather than doing it electronically, you know, moving towards technologically advanced systems that we already have in place." Manual processes, in most cases, can be arranged to follow muscle memory. The Indian way of working is anticipating the problem and grasping your customers' emotion before they can react. The job of a salesperson is a great example that you will find on every nook and corner of Indian towns. They self-train and self-adjust after every conversation they have with their potential customers. No one tells them about the best practices to operate. It is right in their genes. It might be unique for different geographies anyway, but my point here is *practice*. Communication is key for services. And there is a gap in the product knowledge level between the customer service team and the manufacturing team, which hampers a perfect service to the end customer.

I had another encounter of a service industry getting very close to a need to optimize processes. I was part of a company focused on entrepreneurship and innovation for about eight months in Washington, DC, and eventually interned at a New York-based growing start-up called Feather.[81] Feather operates as a Rent-the-Runway for furniture. You can find the most elegant, high-end, expensive furniture pieces for a smaller rental price to adorn your home. So, instead of buying the furniture, you can afford the same high-end furniture at a lower monthly cost. Even though furniture is a tangible product, the company's value addition is in offering rental

---

81. "About Feather," Feather, accessed November 10, 2020.

services with white-glove deliveries, complete with efficient packing, unpacking, and installing. No manufacturing—just assisting consumers with the best-suited set of furniture for their homes and offices. I started in the finance team to look over an inventory model, with my inner operations soul craving to visit the warehouses to observe and share my best practices in Lean.

In the first two weeks of my internship, I visited that Brooklyn warehouse three times. Going there used to prepare me for *Gemba,* which is a Japanese term for "actual place." I remember *Gemba* from my training days at Tata. My trainer there had emphasized a lot on walking down in the actual place of work as many times as possible to find scope of improvement. While taking my warehouse rounds in Brooklyn, I developed many ideas for transforming that small 750-square-foot space into a last mile fulfillment center machine. It never became the meat of my work, though. The team I worked on was only focused on customer conversion. They wanted to expand their customer base online to create a good market presence.

They were also working to create a huge inventory of the best selected items in their inventory. My other work was optimizing the old inventory, thinking of ways to reuse most of it. Among all of this, the team had to deliver on their customer promise of high-quality service and products. Now, there are a hundred ways in which I could have provided "quality service" using that old inventory furniture. But what defines the level of that quality? Is there a way I can optimize my resources to provide that quality service without repeating it or being stingy? I structured my train of thought in one question: Can service industry ever apply Lean the way manufacturing processes do?

I stood in their warehouse looking at the stacked-up boxes of lamps and chair accessories on one side and long sofas and mattresses resting along the wall, leaving a narrow pathway to move to the back of the warehouse. Some tools used to be kept in the front of the warehouse for the quick refurbishment of returned furniture pieces so they could be packed and sent off early next morning. My first reaction was to ask for a visual aid that could tell me what everything meant. What was their "inbound" and what constituted "outbound"? How many people did the refurbishing and packing and what process was used to select the pieces from a stack (FIFO—First in First Out or LIFO—Last in First Out). I shared my views about value chain and visual management with them only to hear that speed of service is what they value the most. Well, when there is organized work, you get speed and accuracy automatically. Their view of Lean was achieving the fastest time of delivery and highest customer acquisition, not worrying about the cost at which it comes.

This is true of many start-ups that are looking to scale in their starting years. The companies generally put their efforts on testing and failing and then testing again. They don't want to stick to a process and play safe. I could see the same thought in my discussions. They would never want to be confined to that small warehouse once they got more business. So, survive with whatever works for the day and move on! This helped me learn one thing about the companies: getting lean works only when you realize you've grown stagnant. In the journey of a start-up, the growth phase is so dynamic that they never need the help of Lean or Agile in their work. Only scrappiness gives you happiness. Unfortunately, the story for other service industries that reach the mature phase of their journey is not the same.

There are some key challenges in service processes compared to manufacturing processes. In a manufacturing process, the raw materials go in and get made in a remote factory, and the customer sees it only at the end. In contrast, in service process, it is the customer who is going through every step. So, the possibilities of the customer seeing the problems and inefficiencies in the whole value chain is very high in the service sector. To understand this further, let's take an example from the financial sector. Consider a bank loan process. Here, the sequence of operations is applying for loan, document submission, negotiations, and final approval, and the customer interacts with the bank throughout these subprocesses.[82] When you enter the bank, you are assisted on the basis of the information that you provide to the financial advisor in front of you. They have never seen you before and will probably never see you again but, at that moment, they completely rely on the agility of their data retrieval from the system once they punch your credentials and account number in their system.

For them to work on your loan process seamlessly, they need to have a strong "levelling" of information between their own branch and the branch where you first opened an account. They also need to verify your details with government authorities, other credit card companies and banks where they can pull your financial history, your employer, your apartment owner, and so on. The product here is the loan and the moving pieces, or "raw material," is all the information that they retrieve from dozens of sources. *You* are the center of that "raw material" and *you* still remain

82. "Loan Process," Success Mortgage Partners Inc, accessed November 11, 2020.

the center of their output. You are sitting right in front of them and want all of this to end in a few minutes because, let's face it, you don't like to spend your free time in a bank! Also, that person right behind you in the queue is giving you tough looks.

Pradeesh Wanniarachchi, COO of the Lean Six Sigma company for the Asia region, explains three reasons important for the service industry to perform better than the product industry. First, in manufacturing, you can plan the process and use tools, and everything is tangible, but in the service industry, it is hard to plan the process. Second is the customer. They are the part and parcel of the entire process from start to end until we get profit. The customer sees everything that happens in front and sometimes even behind the screen. So, the deficiencies are visible to the end user the moment they are made. The third is post-sales service cost. Whatever the defects or damages in service manufacturing does not rectify, there will be some additional costs. At the end of the day, the sales team can deliver a good product and have the right customer with some extra costs, but the service industry cannot afford it every single time.[83]

You can also have a leveled communication setup. Many companies rely on their trainers to cascade everything they have learnt over years of struggle in their business. In my interview with Mr. Pradeesh, who has over ten thousand trained students, he pointed out many things in this respect. Trainees from all businesses and organizations join him for visual simulations. He has many of his students from the software industry worried about information management.

---

83. Pradeesh Wanniarachchi, "Can We Apply Lean Six Sigma in Service Industry?," Linkedin, June 14, 2020.

He interjects, "You worry about your dashboard, your flow, speed of execution, and things like that. Why not your shared folder? Imagine the efficiencies you can get if you have your mailbox nicely arranged so that mail is retrieved quickly."

CHAPTER 7

LEAN PROJECTS | CHALLENGES AND MYTHS

"Lean is a complete waste of time. I would never release a single penny for it in my budget," remarked a CFO of one of the largest hospitality companies in US. I was horrified by this statement, but I had practiced my smiling business face for networking events in my MBA class. I kept a façade of the right amount of corporate smile, but this interaction underlined a huge myth about Lean.

This happened at an MBA career event organized in Houston, Texas. It was one of those conferences where you meet representatives from over four hundred companies, all in the same room. There were big job opportunities to explore and even bigger opportunities if you manage to meet a top-level leader. I had followed this company since the start of my MBA, and the moment I saw that CFO, my eyes beamed, as I thought it was a golden opportunity to shine. Mustering all courage and revising my thirty-second elevator pitch in my mind, I approached the table with an enthusiastic "Hello." Even before I had completed my pitch, one of the representatives got hung on the word "lean." He must have had a terrible experience with it in the past, which showed on his face as he frowned at the mention of the word. I sensed the heat and switched to more cautious words of "change management," "operations excellence," and "Toyota Production System."

The conversation took an unexpected turn, as I didn't realize when the casual talk changed into a full-blown five-minute debate within moments. As I got more inquisitive about them and their views on operations excellence, I found that everyone at that table belonged to the finance team of the company and they had their reservations against Lean. They viewed it as a yearlong activity with no results. They saw it as something that takes a lot of resources and hundreds of meetings and brainstorming sessions but comes down to a little to no bottom-line profit. I agreed with these points but didn't have enough information to dive deeper into their experience with Lean and tell them mine. All I can say is there are some challenges and myths that Lean has faced over the years.

The first challenge is that Lean is not time-bound. It focuses highly on influencing organization culture and remains ever improving in small steps. It is a commitment to roll up your sleeves and change process every time there is a product change or train a new person entering the system. As a manager, when you start doing that, it takes time to change people's minds and for the whole system to abide by the new rules. A project leader needs to ensure that the cultural integrity in the team is never disturbed. If that ever happens, there must be a system of checks and balances to seamlessly integrate the change with the same set of steps used in Lean.

In my personal experience, my conversations with operators while implementing the rules used to be very different than the ones I had during my presentations with my manufacturing head. I understood with time that patience is the key to problem solving. Generally, continuous improvements take a backseat in a production setup, hence it needs to be practiced daily—the same way every good habit takes twenty-one days to stick. Maybe I could have tried a twenty-one-day rule with my implementations, too.

The second challenge of Lean is the resistance to change. Change is hard, and this idea of planning to fail makes the efforts even worse. It is difficult to answer basic questions like, "Why are we doing this? Why aren't we planning to demand the problems and solve the problem correctly? What do we not know, and which piece of the architecture do we not have?" At a production plant, most of the working colleagues that you have are engineers. Engineers don't like change; they like to control things. If an engineer has developed a process or manages an area, it would be difficult to criticize about subtleties of the area around questions like, "Why is that tool located one hundred feet away from the worker?" or "Why does it take ten minutes for everyone to go and get a glass of water?" People generally miss such things, but an eye of a Lean practitioner never misses these things. So, resistance to change suddenly becomes a big problem to even set foot toward the first task to implement Lean.

One of the Lean experts that I interacted with told me about his experience with his clients: "The first few months are excruciating, because it is like giving away your ten year-old favorite T-shirt to make space for your new work shirt." It is a slow and boring, repetitive process that many times gives you a feeling that nothing is moving at all. That is what creates impatience, especially among the financial folks who create budgets for their companies and want to forecast a return on investment. A veteran in the Lean space for twenty years, Bob Rush from Tesla has another pain point with his team. Mr. Rush says, "I have a lot of people do what I call a 'punch card' Lean. So, they get on the web and they find a list of twenty-five best Lean tools. And then they think, 'Well, I did *Kaizen*, check! I did 5S, check!' And they want to go down the line and check it rather than use a tool that was best for the situation. They are happy saying, 'I used a tool that didn't work, but hey, I used a tool!'"

In general practice, the shop floor demands *ruling by exceptions*. This was one of the favorite quotes I heard from my boss at Tata. Nowadays, a lot of managers will go, "Oh yeah, everybody's doing that, that's our new standard work." As an example from the workshop, if there is a process that historically was done in two minutes, they will shrug off saying, "That's it, everybody's going to stick to two minutes, so maybe I'll just stick with those 120 seconds too." If there comes an outlier of a figure of seventy seconds, I would be interested in looking at what happened which made it work at seventy seconds. Then, we're all going to do it in seventy seconds by figuring out the technology or method to achieve it. Once the process achieves a better way of functioning in seventy seconds, maybe they can find a way to horizontally apply it in other places as well. This is how an "exceptional process" triggers an improvement.

The third challenge Lean faces is stickiness to standard process. When you try to optimize a process, you spend the maximum time defining the problem. It is the analysis part where you start with a step-by-step implementation and refinement of your solution. Lean goes with the flow and needs to be established fast and loose. Rishav explains his challenge in creating such a change at Faraday Future and Canoo, "One needs to decide between opening this pandora box at the start or waiting till the company starts creating a positive bottom line. The tricky part is, if you don't do that you will make a mistake that would cost tens of thousands of dollars. Right now, it's like, 'Oh, the mistake costs me only twenty bucks and I'll use a simple solution to have this fix the error.' But when it's ten thousand parts you can't fix there. You have to have done it right the first time."[84, 85]

The fourth challenge is convincing everyone to see that the process they are using is not the most efficient way to do things. Often times, it might involve putting effort to break people out of the mindset that they are doing great. Everyone loves the feeling that they are succeeding. In both the manufacturing and the service industry, this often comes from creating a stable environment that hits its key metrics and can run smoothly and consistently day in and day out. This has to be done keeping a larger goal of organizational success in mind. One thing that can surely ruin a team is criticizing a person who is putting in efforts. If you ask someone who has achieved a clean workplace to look around and see how much waste they are living in, it might backfire their productivity.

This would be a shock as it challenges their efforts and feeling of success. Most of the time, this happens between a team and their managers, or maybe an over-demanding

---

84. "Faraday Future: Experience a New Species," Faraday Future, accessed October 6, 2020.

85. "Canoo: Electric Lifestyle, Sport and Working Vehicles," Canoo, accessed October 6, 2020.

leader. This challenge is often overcome by using a third-party perspective. External advisors and consultants are expected to be the third set of eyes for the company's operations. What ends up happening is a quick review of the work and creating a long list of wishful decisions, out of which maybe 10 to 20 percent get fulfilled, keeping rest of them in a limbo. This is a famous joke among consultants that clients who hire them for making strategic recommendations hardly come back for implementations.

Example of a Government Office

A major challenge that causes misalignment is when the decisions and changes are made in silos. The teams are mostly devoid of input from others or consideration for the system as a whole, which can quickly deteriorate efficiencies, relationships, and profits.

Tony Ingelido has thirty years of experience working in healthcare and multiple other places in federal government. He shared some stories about working with some frontline staff in healthcare and trying to help them understand the importance of waste in the operations. It is a good example of a service industry environment. Tony's team dealt with senior citizens because it was a long-term care facility. A lot of his colleagues didn't have any clue about Lean. They recognized and just believed inherently that there was waste in their day-to-day work and that the "system" was to blame. They accepted the fact that things were inefficient, and it was just the way it was going to be! This turns out even worse when, due to such inherent inefficiencies, organizations feel the need to hire more people. That's what happened in his case. It was tough to get people to understand that how Lean concepts, if implemented correctly, can impact the bottom line and how they impact the ability to maybe pay more or have money for training and provide a good raise for your employees!

Mr. Ingelido was able to get a lot done through training. He implemented a lot of little training programs to get people to understand aspects of their jobs that lead to inefficiency. The area was filled with mundane processes like paperwork processing, not being able to find stationary, delay in prints and copies, etc. Yes, these trivial jobs can sometimes take days in follow-up and completion. For those project managers out there, remember days when you have to do long, ten-email exchanges with a team just to get a document revised or get an approval for some work? We all do it in the name of organized work and seamless progress. That's a big thing in any of these service industries—you know you're putting things in the right place or the basic tool of the five S's of Lean. Mr. Ingelido agrees to the fact that while government offices are still far behind in terms of the basic awareness, this is changing with digitization of offices. It is like taking a quantum jump after long years of stagnation.

The Leadership Perspective

In a survey done by AlixPartners with industry leaders, only 30 percent of the leaders agreed to getting over 5 percent financial savings from Lean projects. This is such a meager result considering the rest of the 70 percent respondents never realized any savings or results as low as less than 5 percent savings from their Lean projects. From the same survey, it comes out that a lack of effective management and governance is the biggest roadblock in most failures.[86]

When dealing with company leadership, a challenge with consultants is the lack of scenario creating a void between the actual situation and what the client company actually wants them to do. Consultants normally start their work at the top of the ladder with C-level leadership and have to prove the worth of a project.[87] Most of the time, this "worth" falls under the financial lines, and consultants are under pressure to show a bottom line improvement in a short time. That's not why you do Lean. This clash results in "lost milestones" and eventually inaction and abandonment of the project altogether.

Bob Rush, who has done this work for the past thirty years, mentions this pain: "I've gone to CEOs that are adamant that Lean doesn't work and it's Japanese work, not applicable to their industry. We tried it at my last company, and it'll never work. And then there are stories that they tell about how well their operations are and how much they have achieved in the last many years without even considering Lean." Many times, these situations digress a consultant's attention. They have an additional task of convincing the leadership that their methods are effective. It is similar to the situation if you go to a doctor for an illness and he suggests you take a drug for it. However, because you are arguing, he has to convince you that his suggestions are effective. You want to get well, but you don't trust the doctor.

---

86. Zach Bastin, Albert Sang and Ashrae Sahni, "There is no Quick Pay-off from Lean," AlixPartners, September 15, 2020

87. Ruben Cornelissen, "What are the main challenges when implementing lean and how do industry and company characteristics influence these challenges?," Wageningen University, November 23 2013.

Mr. Rush continues, "I like to work at the uppermost level and the most direct level. So, I want to be with the CEO and his staff, and then I want to be with the associates, whether they're building a product, designing a product, or coding. I had a semiconductor company as a client. This leader was adamant of his ways and was a hard convert. *It was one of my failures.* Now I've learned the personality type that I'll work with immediately and maybe try to convey a hard 'no' right from the start if there is a mismatch in our personalities."

The last challenge is about the misconceptions attached to the results of Lean. People in the lower rungs have a constant fear of job loss while implementing Lean projects. There have been numerous times when I used to visit my team in the assembly line to take a stop-watch study of processes and people would start to work slower. From their history with multiple initiatives and how supervisors functioned, they knew it for a fact that if they worked quickly, they became more "efficient'" and could then be handed over with more work. If there was any scope of improving the process, it would lead to removal of manpower from the workshop. This is the point where right communication builds promise and trust.

Mr. Ingelido also led continuous improvement initiatives both as a leader in the Department of Treasury in Virginia and later consulting for the DoD (Department of Defense). He has a similar observation in the processes he led. He states that every time he invited his client's leaders to come forward and speak to their workers directly, it helped clarify most of these misconceptions.

There is a solution to the above problems. Does it need to change? I hope not. Any process change would be as slow as what it is today. A change is excruciating for the workers and takes longer time to show results. Does it need to evolve? Heck yes! Evolution would mean using tools that change the system at large and don't depend on incremental changes. The best way to evolve is to use technology.

The future holds a separate set of challenges for Lean. With IoT (Internet of Things) installed in warehouses and multiple production setups, it may come to a need for an expanded IT infrastructure, new sources of downtime from service outages, the possibility of data overload, the addition of technical staff members, the possibility of less flexibility to change, new communication complexities, and data security concerns.[88] I come across a lot of new job profiles for data server managers for companies like Google and Microsoft. These are completely new jobs whose sole purpose is to keep the servers up and running. When you have everything transitioning to the internet, the nature of risks changes and data needs to be secured to keep things "lean."

So, while we have a lot of challenges, there are solutions to tackle with awareness issues and myths about Lean's effectiveness. The first step is to identify the problem. Working on finding the root cause wins half the battle for you. By giving it a name and description, you are empowering individuals with knowledge so that they can begin a journey of self-discovery. Once they know what to look for, they will then find waste themselves. From there, it is almost a certainty that they will want to eliminate the waste as quickly as possible so as to keep their otherwise perfect process from blemish. Seeing waste is a skill developed through practice. Remember, *Kaizen* is forever. Show them where the path starts and let

88. "The Internet of Things: Mapping the Value Beyond the Hype," McKinsey Global Institute. June 2015.

the allure of a better future draw them down to it. Once the team knows the problem, it is all about finding the right Lean tool to use instead of checking the boxes for all available tools and practicing "punch-card Lean."

Another way is the age-old carrot and stick method. It works perfectly with many tools used in Lean. In a supply chain, for example, a vendor and a company have service level agreements (SLAs) to maintain and uphold a certain performance level. Most SLAs have an indemnity clause (indemnity means money).[89] The indemnity clause functions as a guarantee that the terms of the contract will be upheld by incentivizing success and penalizing failure. This sort of arrangement drives the key function of the Lean process. By incentivizing success, a vendor is encouraged to do better what they already do best, and the company that contracts with them thus receives an excellent product on time and in exactly the right amount.

---

89. Stephanie Overby, Lynn Greiner and Lauren Gibbons Paul, "What is an SLA? Best practices for service-level agreements," *CIO*, July 5, 2017.

CHAPTER 8

CASE 2 | GROUND REALITIES—BOEING'S LEAN IMPLEMENTATION

———

Boeing is one of the world's largest aircraft manufacturers.[90] I have always considered building an aircraft to be the highest level of manufacturing challenge. It is more about the risks and their potential consequences of failure which makes aircraft-manufacturing a work of precision and accuracy. A Boeing 737 fits around six hundred thousand different parts together in its assembly process. Think of the chaos it creates in the operations system and the pressure teams undergo to create a symphony out of that chaos.[91]

I came across a story in one of my interviews. Mr. Gary Weber, a former Lean expert at Boeing, describes how the company used Lean to improve its processes in the early 2000s, the challenges teams faced, and the loss of jobs faced

———

90. "Historical Snapshot," Boeing, accessed October 29, 2020.
91. Ibid.

by employees as a by-product of the implemented system. Gary worked in Boeing for over five years and, for the most part, learnt and implemented multiple Lean tools in his projects.

Gary was there when Boeing 737 was being built. Think of a huge production facility with different workstations complete with tools, equipment, and engineers posted to work on the aircraft. There were about sixteen to twenty stations all in a single line with unfinished aircraft sitting on each of those stations. Instead of a head-to-tail arrangement, every airplane was diagonally parked in the final assembly area to save space. A standard conveyor moving line is where the vehicle is oriented from nose to tail. But you turn them on a forty-five-degree angle into a parking spot. That's how they were aligned on every station. So, it was kind of a parallel parking. That's where they sat for an entire day during the production hours. Most of the production work, including fitting of parts, testing, and quality checks happened during the day. At night, the second shift had a different set of workers who pulled one aircraft at a time, moved it into the next position, and parked it. Then they pulled the next one into the next position and parked it. That's all what they did on the second shift—move all the planes to the next position, which took a lot of time and effort. So, essentially, what the operations team would have is sixteen hours of jobs at that one parking spot in one day.

Many of the technicians and mechanics were so good at their job that they would finish their job in five hours and go home because they knew the planes were never going to be moved to the next station in the rest of the time. They were not going to have another plane in that position until tomorrow, so they worked four to five hours to complete their job, went home, and got paid full for that day. That was the way they had worked since World War II.

Boeing had started with some Lean implementation for which it enlisted a Japanese coach. This coach was Gary's *Sensei* (Japanese for "teacher") and had visited them to teach Lean concepts. When he came to that plant, he noticed the extra work and chaos right away. Now, we are talking about the plane that's the number one selling airplane in the world. Not one company sold more than the number of 737 Boeing sold at that time. It is still a real cash cow for Boeing. At that time, it took about 900,000 hours to build one of those planes. This was improved to 5,500 aircraft unit hours and it has dropped again to 4,000 now.[92] Even if we just consider the manpower deployed to cover those hours, that converts to a lot of money in production costs! The *Sensei* came in and he was a giant of a person in the community of Lean practitioners. He's the one most spoken up in the book *Lean Thinking*, so when he spoke, people listened. He was stern in his demeanor and demanded discipline.

When the *Sensei* was called, he went into that plant and talked to the general manager of operations at Boeing. The general manager of that plant was Carolyn, the first woman ever appointed to that position. For 1990s, that's a pretty big thing. She was elevated through engineering; she earned the place, and everyone knew it. When the *Sensei* spoke to her and said "You need to make a moving line here," Gary happened to be there and heard that entire conversation. A moving line was a whole different ball game. It meant that aircraft would be produced while it was being moved forward simultaneously. It would completely remove the second shift

---

92. Chris Brady, "Production," The Boeing 737 Technical Site, September 1999.

of aircraft pushers. The challenge was to achieve precision of work in that moving scenario.

"We're not Toyota, we don't make cars," Carolyn said about the *Sensei's* suggestion. He said, "How does that matter?" and pointed over the standing airplane, exclaiming, "They're still on wheels!"

It was not completely true because part of that assembly line was not on wheels, but he was right. Most of it was still on the wheels. And he mentioned this because he knew there were ways to work around the setup to make it more agile. She didn't believe the *Sensei's* arrogance. He was coming in the plant for the first time and wanted her to set up a moving conveyor line just like Toyota. She said, "You don't own stock in this company. You don't know the risks."

They had a brief back and forth and got pretty aggravated with each other. She sent him off saying, "You come and talk to me when you own part of this company." A few days after the general manager had issued her challenge, the *Sensei* returned. Striding over to her desk, he slapped down a piece of paper. It was a stock certificate for eight thousand shares of Boeing. The stock at that time was selling at $100 a share, so this represented an investment of $800,000.

"Now we are building a moving line." The general manager had no choice but to go along with it.

"You realize that if this doesn't work, I'll be fired," she said. "You should be fired if you don't do this," he replied.

Gary saw them having this conversation at the end of that day after he was done taking a tour of the facility. It was a brilliant military maneuver. Carolyn had developed faith in the *Sensei,* as he convinced her with the level of risk he could take. She said, "I'm committed 100 percent." That changed everything. It took them some quick months until they had a moving line there. They had a big celebration when the first plane went through the complete assembly without stopping. She was heralded as a hero for the company.

Gary didn't realize at the time, but the general manager's commitment was indeed complete. It was terrible for the other managers and supervisors on the assembly line as well because they had to attend workshop-after-workshop on the floor to enforce things. Every workshop Gary had included had the *Sensei* with him, accompanied by an interpreter, and there were many storming events that used to happen every day in those workshops. Many times, the *Sensei* would ask some really tough questions and exercises, which would completely change the way of doing things.

There was another facet to this—Boeing had a union shop. If its workers decided they didn't want to be a part of anything, it wouldn't work. In fact, they would do whatever they could to delay any effort to make an improvement. There was a hiccup in the improvement journey between the union and the management. *Sensei's* team was making a lot of improvements there, and the CEO announced that the company had reduced that 900,000 hours per aircraft by 30 percent, which is staggering by any standard. In addition, to the horror of those hardworking people, the CEO went on TV, the local news, and broadcasted that he was going to have a layoff because the company had reduced hours by 30 percent.[93]

That didn't go well with the union. Gary was tasked as the manager of those union workers implementing Lean in the assembly line. Two days later, Gary stood on the shop floor trying to arrange another workshop. He was talking

93. Shawn Tully, "Boeing Must Transform the Way It Builds Planes," *Fortune*, March 8, 1993.

with the union people on the shop floor, but they didn't pay any heed to him anymore. The major divide was the interpretation of this productivity improvement. With the tools he learned from his *Sensei*, Gary was looking to make a 50 percent improvement and in the union's mind, that meant 50 percent people being laid off. That was a tragic error in that announcement by the CEO. But Carolyn, the general manager, stood up for those union people. She walked through them and committed that she would resign if any of them is laid off. It was very powerful.

The union contract was up in a year. Everyone knew for certain there was going to be a strike. And it was going to be awful. The general manager's commitment also included that she would fight to the end for them to have their jobs retained. They were angry that they did not have the chance to be a manager of the continuous improvement, similar to what Gary was doing—to be the leader of these improvements. Their union contract did not lay out a position for that. The GM swore she would do whatever she could to earn their trust and she created a position for the union, exactly as they wanted.

Pretty soon, Boeing cut up the floor into sections. There were six sections, separate teams were made, and they named their own team. This would bring some great dynamic change on the production floor. They started developing their own plans and Gary was the one actually training those union guys to be the leaders that would eventually replace him. This was a huge change but a right thing to do. People who know how to build the plant should be the ones leading the improvements.

The last challenge was to bridge the divide between the pro-American group listening to a Japanese person. There were a number of times that the union forces did not follow the instructions and stalled the workshops. Using Japanese terminology was somewhat abrasive to them. Gary learned very quickly not to use Japanese terms like *Muda*, and they were not a fan of Japanese way of defining things in those terms. The *Sensei* was an eighty-year-old man. He was a believer of the facts and action. There were people on the factory floor whose father had died in the World War II. This whole issue is big. *Sensei* started relating with those union workers on that level. His passion proved that he was there to help the team learn and grow. Soon, Gary noticed that slowly and gradually, the Americans understood the passion that *Sensei* carried. They got over that eventually. They started listening and saw the wisdom in the *Sensei* as well, in the sense they started understanding the difference between American culture, and they started celebrating with the Japanese when they had even a small success. Those celebrations developed a special bond that helped the team accomplish the Lean transformation faster.

PART 3

CHAPTER 9

THE NEW OIL | IN DATA WE TRUST?

———

In God we trust, all others must bring data.

—W. EDWARDS DEMING

Data is a powerful means to drive business in today's world. Many of you have experienced it firsthand not only professionally, but also as a means to socialize. You want to learn a new skill? Boom! There are three different apps that help you learn. Oh, so you're looking for a new relationship? There's an app that is running all kinds of data sets on your personal preferences, online history, your last visited destination, and the last piece of clothing you searched on Amazon.[94] It can be seen in industrial use, too—instead of supply chain managers depending on their phones to keep a tab on a latest

---

94. Rebecca Heilweil, "Tinder may not get you a date. It will get your data," *Vox*, February 14, 2020.

consignment travelling in a truck, they can rely on bar codes and RFIDs to track it digitally while they focus on more important stuff. The applications might seem easy, but there are layers of refinement that data undergoes before providing actionable insights.

As easy it is for the online apps to collect and develop insights from their online database, traditional companies struggle to make sense of their data. They are being constantly helped by a team of consultants, both internal and external, to be digitally transformed. The COVID-19 pandemic that started in the first half of 2020 showed the world firsthand how being digital is a necessity for the future.[95] There is hardly any company that didn't suffer a dip in their revenues and sales without quickly jumping onto the bandwagon of e-commerce and promotion on digital platforms. Going digital means creating a new pillar in the company, which not only develops new capabilities of capturing, refining, and analyzing data, but also helps cut across the organization to help transform everything with data as a base.

In June 2020, I completed an externship with AT&T and had a chance to attend a webinar on customer focus by Tiffani Bova. She is a growth and innovation evangelist at Salesforce who also is a real-time influencer on digital transformation, the future of work, and sales excellence. In the webinar, she stressed the real application of data.[96] She remarked, "Everyone says data is the new oil. But is it?" Comparing data with oil in many ways is accurate. We are

95. Aamer Beg, Bryce Hall, Paul Jenkins, Eric Lamarre and Brian McCarthy, "The COVID-19 recovery will be digital: A plan for the first 90 days," McKinsey Digital, May 14, 2020.

96. Tiffany Bova, "Customer Focus with Tifanny Bova" (Webinar, AT&T Externship 2020, Online, July 15, 2020)

using it as a commodity in our work. In many ways, we are surrounded by data, but I have always wondered whether just keeping data is enough. She continues,

> *"It is similar to saying you extract the oil in Texas and put it directly in your car. But, that's not how it happens. You need to refine the oil, put in additives to make gas and then you use it. Analytics acts as a refinery for our data. And, until you create some business insights out of it, you cannot use data as oil."*[97]

How remarkable! This analogy goes a long way into everything you do while measuring a process, too. Using a tool and identifying the problem is just the beginning, even though the right identification of the root cause solves half of the issue, itself. The most common technique that Lean practitioners use is called the "5-Why Analysis." The method is as it sounds: for every defect or mistake that you are dealing with, ask the reason it happened. And then ask again why that situation arose in the first place. Then go another step back by asking the third why and so on. Most of the time, you don't have to go beyond the third why, but it is recommended to explore up to five steps back. Once, you get to the root cause, you collect data to verify it, check whether it is happening in other locations or with other processes.[98] Then you go for an internal benchmarking, identifying metrics and measures that you might be using internally someplace else that can solve the problem. If not, you explore external

---

97. Ibid.
98. "5 Whys: The Ultimate Root Cause Analysis Tool," Kanbanize, accessed February 20, 2021.

solutions. Data plays a crucial role in giving you a metric and a target to reach to prevent the problem in the future.

The development of data proficiency has been gradual over the past two decades. Early examples of big data analytics were largely confined to digitally available data. You have an equipment, you get the data, and then run it to get some patterns or conclusions. IoT opened up the physical world. Perhaps, the most striking example is in manufacturing. Manufacturers are already using IoT sensors in conjunction with big data analytics in preventive maintenance of their machinery. This is still a narrow use but as more of the business becomes connected and its big data platform is expanded, the use of data analysis will cover the entire enterprise.[99]

For now, the next step for manufacturers is shifting from simply using predictive analytics for machinery to analyzing the entire production environment, identifying skill gaps by analyzing production methodology shift patterns. It also changes with the digital prototyping of new processes to reduce waste and engaging in an optimization program that gets performed in even tighter circles with everyone collaborating on the same data set at every stage.[100]

Data and Digital Lean

In further chapters, we will discuss the new avatar of Lean called digital Lean. It has huge leverage to be chosen as the likely next heir to the traditional Lean philosophy just

99. Prema Srinivasan, "How to Use Big Data Analytics to Supercharge Lean Manufacturing," PTC, September 3, 2020.
100. Ibid.

because of the infusion of data as a new commodity. When we talk about digital Lean implementation, it has a high dependence on data management. It generally requires three key enablers at a production plant, and every plant would have different immediate needs across the three areas:

1. *Collating data: Collaboration of IT and Operations Tech (OT)*—Prior to Industry 4.0, information technology (IT) and operational technology (OT) acted like two distinct application areas with little to no overlap. By moving deeper into data processing, digital Lean enables an integration of IT and OT (control systems, industrial networks, ERP), which brings plant and operations data to business users.[101]

2. *Standardizing the processes*—Plant processes generate data that serves as input for digital Lean. But if processes are not carried out with standardization and discipline, accurate and continuous data cannot be obtained. As a result, the impact of a digital Lean initiative would be muted. Key in this regard is the role of plant leadership in defining and enforcing processes to ultimately provide more accurate data.

3. *Application of data: Data-enabled technology platforms*—As important as IT and OT collaboration and disciplined process and data management are, relevant technological platforms should be leveraged to truly harness the benefits of digital Lean. When choosing a technology platform, such as a digital twin, organizations should be sure to consider factors such as

---

101. Scott Birch, "Deloitte: scaling digital technologies in manufacturing," Manufacturing Global, October 2, 2020.

platform flexibility, integration with other systems, and data administration.[102]

There are various use cases of these three factors, which are combined with data analysis tools in the industries. For example, a pharmaceutical company wanted to get to the root causes of variability in an important production process. Operators suspected that some fifty variables were involved but couldn't determine the relationships among them to improve overall efficiency. Working closely with data specialists, the operators used neural networks (a machine-learning technique) to model the potential combinations and effects of the variables. After standardizing their collated data, they ultimately determined that five of them mattered most. Once the primary drivers were clear, the operators focused their efforts on optimizing the relevant parameters and then managing them as part of routine plant operations. This helped the company to improve yields by 30 percent.[103]

Similarly, a leading steel producer used advanced analytics to identify and capture margin-improvement opportunities worth more than $200 million a year across its production value chain.[104] This result is noteworthy because the company already had a fifteen-year history of deploying Lean approaches and had recently won an award for quality and process excellence. The steelmaker began with a data analysis method called the Monte Carlo simulation, which is widely used in biology, computational physics, engineering,

102. Ibid.
103. Rajat Dhawan, Kunvar Singh, Ashish Tuteja, "When big data goes lean," McKinsey & Company, February 1, 2014.
104. Ibid.

finance, and insurance to model ranges of possible outcomes and their probabilities.

Monte Carlo simulations are used to model the probability of different outcomes in a process that cannot easily be predicted due to the presence of random variables. It is a technique used to understand the impact of risk and uncertainty in prediction and forecasting models.[105] Manufacturing companies can adapt these methods to model their own uncertainties by running thousands of simulations using historical plant data to identify the probabilities of breakdowns, as well as variations in cycle times and in the availability of multiple pieces of equipment across parts of a production process.

The steelmaker focused on what it thought was the principal bottleneck in an important process, where previous continuous improvement efforts had already helped raise output by 10 percent. When statisticians analyzed the historical data, they recognized that the process suffered from multiple bottlenecks, which shifted under different conditions. The part of the process that the operators traditionally focused on, had a 60 percent probability of causing problems, but two other parts could also cripple output, though they were somewhat less likely to do so.[106]

Customer feedback and feedforward are also important when we move a step ahead on the external customers front. With apps being predominant in generating a one-click order, it becomes important to make the order fulfillment through apps even faster and more accurate. As an example, if there are more chocolates getting sold during February's second

105. "Monte Carlo Simulation," IBM Education, accessed February 27, 2021.
106. Rajat Dhawan, Kunvar Singh, Ashish Tuteja, ibid.

week, (more specifically, Valentine's week), then that's what should get restocked and picked by the robots. Conversely, if the people in California prefer oranges over grapefruits, this fact would be used by the demand planning team to stock more oranges. Moreover, that trigger from the forecast generated by the demand planning team should match with the actual data from the robots describing which product they picked the most in a certain period for California customers.

Visual Tool for Manufacturing—Embedded Analytics

The analysis of big data sets generated in the manufacturing process can minimize production defects and keep quality standards high, while at the same time increasing efficiency, wasting less time, and saving more money. There are several tools that could be described here for the sake of clarity of data-dependence. But, when it is seen from the perspective of operations excellence, there are some specific ones that demand our attention. In addition to the Neural networks done with the healthcare example or the Monte Carlo simulation, embedded analytics is a technique valuable for manufacturing.

Embedded analytics is the integration of analytic content and capabilities within applications, such as business process applications. Terms that you hear in supply chains like CRM (customer relationship management) or ERP (enterprise resource planning) are all examples of embedded analytics.[107] Their goal is to help users work smarter by

---

107. Adam Murray, "How Can Manufacturing Data Help Your Organization?," Sisense, January 13, 2020.

incorporating relevant data and analytics into business processes and work more efficiently as these capabilities merge with their applications used every day. This is in contrast to traditional business intelligence, or the "BI" data visualizations, which focuses on extracting insight from data within the silo of analysis.

Embedded analytics are particularly valuable in terms of quality control and optimizing manufacturing efficiency. Computerized and automated monitoring systems used in it are far more sensitive and accurate than the human eye and capture discrepancies more accurately and cheaply in real time. This continuous, smart, machine-based scrutiny significantly decreases the number of tests essential to maintain quality parameters.[108] Data can also be used to calculate the probabilities of delays and to identify, develop, and implement backup plans.

Embedded analytics is also faster and more autonomous than traditional data analysis. Analytic technology embedded within machinery can do the job at the point of data generation. So, less manual intervention is necessary, and decisions can be influenced directly by data. The processes, in turn, are accelerated, using fewer resources. Effectively, big data enables manufacturers to improve and streamline their processes across production and quality control.

Variability is another big problem in a manufacturing setup. There is a constant tussle between flexibility and stability in a production plant. An ideal plant has a great balance between the two. By segmenting the manufacturing process into clusters of related production activities and analyzing

---

108. "What is Embedded Analytics?," Logi Analytics, accessed February 28, 2021.

the data to show interdependencies, it is possible to identify stages in the process that influence the variability in yield.[109] Addressing variability can increase the yield by a value of millions of dollars per product.

Big data is a huge part of Industry 4.0, and that is where most of the industries are trying to move in the eventual step of digital transformation. It is still far away but it can be a start of industry 5.0, where people just move away from the production lines and everything gets controlled by a software. We would have engineers just working on this software and not worrying about the physical aspects of the equipment. It is still far away but it will be something inspired from the Pareto principle—80 percent of the giant section of software and only 20 percent of the physical aspects of machines and the eventual implementation.[110]

---

109. Ibid.
110. Kevin Kruse, "The 80/20 Rule and How it Can Change Your Life," *Forbes*, March 7, 2016.

CHAPTER 10

THE POTENTIAL
OF AI AND ML

—

In 2016, there was a huge uproar when AlphaGo, an AI bot from Google, challenged world champion Lee Sedol from South Korea in the board game of Go.[111] It is considered to be one of the most complex in the history of board games. It has also been used in mathematical research due to the sheer number of possible moves on it. Every game lasts only one hundred and fifty moves between experts on a standard 19x19 sized board. To give a perspective, there are 10,000,000, 000,000,000,000,000,000,000 ways to move on a small 5x5 board.[112] The game of Go is hard to automate because of the sheer randomness of the game. A team at Google decided to try their artificial intelligence prowess by creating AlphaGo, a software that can think and play the game on its own.

However, Google faced a special challenge here. The team had no way of knowing if the coding it had written

111. Christof Koch, "How the Computer Beat the Go Master," *Scientific American*, March 19, 2016, Accessed October 27, 2020.
112. Ibid.

would ever reach the level of intellect that Lee had in the game. There was a five-match series played between Lee and AlphaGo. After starting strong, Lee started gradually faltering on the game and ultimately lost four out of the five games. This sent huge shockwaves among the people of Korea, who adore their champion. After the match, the team of twenty from DeepMind, the original company, revealed that this was not the full potential to which the bot was prepared. It was just a prototype, not even a beta version or an alpha version. The team was eyeing healthcare with its AI creations and was seriously invested in this endeavor. There could be more improvements in AlphaGo.[113] That day, AI was proven to be all-powerful, in a subtle but a big way!

When we think of digital, an obvious image of automatic processes comes to mind. Artificial intelligence (AI) and machine learning (ML) are the tools which catapult our imagination for the next era's process automation. To give a brief introduction of the concepts here: artificial intelligence is any task that a machine can perform accurately and smartly, on its own. Chat boxes that pop up on a website, a new friend recommendation on your social media page, or a nudge email to you to get that Louis Vuitton purse because you bought a dress are all examples of AI reading your behaviors and acting on them. Machine learning is a part of AI, which in very basic terms lets the machine learn with the data fed to it. So, does Lean need AI? Or vice versa? Short answer is "it depends."

In a recent global CEO survey done by PwC, 85 percent of the CEOs agree that AI will bring significant changes in the

113. Alex Irpan, "AlphaGo vs Lee Sedol: Post Match Commentaries," *Sorta Insightful* (blog), March 17, 2016.

way they do business in the next five years.[114] Digital operations has already taken its course to become consumer-centric, but accountability and exploitability of its decisions still remains a concern among 84 percent of those CEOs.[115] That concern magnifies when we are talking about technological changes in people-heavy manufacturing organizations. When I discuss AI in a production factory or a product development process, the impact mostly comes out in the initial stages of the development.[116] This is the time when the teams are trying to identify the need or want from the customer to design a solution. Initial stages are really critical to determine whether the idea that you are working on is actually viable or not. In other words, it is the product-proving or customer-product fit phase.

In many cases, when the company needs to be quick on proving process or needs to launch an improvement quickly, they release a "beta" version to a limited population to get a grasp on the performance. This not only saves them the time to search for test-consumers or on standard surveys, but also provides them a credible voice of customer to improve their product.[117] This quick turnaround sounds easy but in reality, it is complex. Most startups don't get their hands-on multiple customers already using a product and cannot release a beta version to them. Many times, the product is brand new

114. Andrew Quibell, "Lean Management Meets Artificial intelligence, Machine Learning, the Internet of All Things," Lean Enterprise Institute, April 16, 2018.

115. Ibid.

116. Stephen Laaper and Brian Keifer, "Digital lean manufacturing—Industry 4.0 technologies transform lean processes to advance the enterprise," Deloitte Insights, August 21, 2020.

117. Alex Bousetta, "Does Lean Six Sigma need AI and ML?" LinkedIn, August 21, 2018.

and needs to be tested for the very first time. In those cases, simulations are really useful.

Machine learning algorithms are an application of artificial intelligence. The algorithms are specifically designed to learn from what input we provide to them. The most recent interesting applications are online games and thinking hats for many network optimization tools that use machine learning.[118] It just means they are pulling out data from the past or from studying your moves in the game (like AlphaGo) and making decisions themselves without any person's help. MLs understand additional information and provide responses based on those inputs. Many software programs are developed using such simulation.

For example, Cruise Automation, a subsidiary of GM, is developing self-driving cars on the west coast.[119] They have been unable to bring their cars outside to check for the safety software programs they have installed. But autonomous cars need those experience miles to vet for their effectiveness in real driving scenarios. MLs help them get those miles by running the software in simulated situations. But does it all require any contribution from the Lean processes? I came across a documentary which simplifies the integration of AI/ML with the Lean world. A concept called the "Johari window" segregates our knowledge and awareness of different items and helps evaluate the problems from an outside perspective.[120] The concept is predominantly used for teams

---

118. Anand Rao, Flavio Palaci, and Wilson Chao, "This is what the world's CEOs really think of AI," World Economic Forum, June 25, 2019.
119. "The integrated engineering challenge of our generation," Cruise Automation, accessed October 31, 2020.
120. Ruby Rumsen, "The Johari Window," *E-Learning Network* (blog), February 15, 2018.

and the information we know about each individual in the team to avoid any blind spots in the team. But we can borrow the concept for a second here to see how our knowledge lies for any project—we divide our knowledge into known knowns (something we already know), known unknowns (something that we know that we need to explore more) and unknown unknowns (the blind spots and what we have no ability of knowing). In Lean, three scenarios for product or process design can be considered to see how Lean tools need to be used:

1. Known knowns: For the functions that are to be automated, are the key process parameters fully known? If the answer is yes, we just need to stabilize the process, using traditional Lean and Lean Six Sigma tools. What this means is, without parameters, it is not possible to measure the end goal and we have to start from the basic step of defining our goals first.

2. Known Unknowns: Using the Lean Six Sigma methodology, did we discover the key process parameters, and can we model them? If so, we need to adjust the process parameters based on statistical tools, such as regressions. Regressions are methods to correlate multiple factors and find out which of those factors actually moves the needle for our parameters.

3. Unknown unknowns: Is the model too complex to establish now or with time due to the number of parameters, unknown parameters or changing parameters with time? This is where machine learning comes to play. Based on available data, it allows us to adjust the process or assist as a decision support system.

Successful organizations are those that already have some kind of "digital operations teams." This might span across disciplines and functions, responsible for designing the digital assets, applications, and platforms needed to support the business model. The capability to slice and dice the data into more meaningful chunks of useful facts is an underutilized muscle in the industrial sector. Most businesses only use a fraction of the benefit from the data they hold.[121] The trick is having the vision to see how the data can be manipulated that helps frame tomorrow's customer need and expectation beyond today's norm.

Smart working with smart technologies will push start-ups and entrepreneurs to adapt to the Lean management to compete with the changing and innovative business transformation.

Bill of Materials—Application of AI

One application for AI is working with a bill of materials for multiple products. A bill of materials (BOM) is a list of raw materials that contains a description of each part, the supplier's name, the SKU number, and specifications of that part, arranged line by line and shared with everyone in the team to keep track of the raw materials being put in the product. In a perfect world, every SKU would have its own BOM.[122] SKU is stock keeping unit. Simply put, every unique item that you store in the warehouse counts as one SKU. For example, if you have five teddy bears in different colors and

---

121. Ibid.

122. Jose Arturo Garza-Reyes, "The Future of Manufacturing—Industry 4.0," The Future Factory, accessed February 21, 2021.

design, all five of them would be counted as separate SKUs and they would all have their own bill of materials. With every improvement or a cost reduction activity that takes place, the BOM needs to be updated.

The traditional way that this BOM is updated in typical manufacturing setups is using manual enterprise resource planning (ERP) platforms like SAP, which saves this database with all the specific details together with a few licensed holders.[123] It takes an effort for those few people managing the SAP software to retrieve, edit, and update the details of tens of thousands of SKUs in BOM every day. All of this manual work is covered through multiple people being recruited in the department to manage this data. An integrated system helps the operations team collate everything together. It will be more of an integration of the software with people who are implementing it. Every supply chain team's ultimate goal is to match every part mentioned on the list with the one actually fitted on the product. This integration is a form of digital Lean. Industry 4.0 and AI help to provide more accurate, precise, and timely information about operations. It not only helps realize Lean principles but also increases the impact of core Lean tools, such as *Kanban*. Moreover, the increased availability of high-frequency data from Industry 4.0 technologies, coupled with growing processing power, has led to quicker and deeper insights from BOM details that were virtually impossible several years ago.[124]

It has to be ensured that a BOM material list is absolutely right; only then can the AI assimilate all the different BOMs and all the different parts that are fitted in various products.

123. Ibid.
124. Ibid.

That's more difficult for us and it takes a lot more research for us to figure out. For example, if you need a washer, how many other SKUs use that washer? It will also help define the *Kanban* process. So, I can really assimilate that information very quickly and tell you how many Kanban you need at the moment and how many of them would be in the pipeline safety stock. Now, this would have an impact on other horizontal teams working with you. I would need to incorporate the quality system to understand which supplier is best for the washer and which supplier can be allocated for the required demand.

The most common metric that the BOM manager discusses with suppliers and his own supply chain team is BOM accuracy.[125] For many companies dealing in complex projects like assembling an airplane or developing a motorbike, this percentage (BOM accuracy percentage) varies between 85 to 95 percent. This means that up to 15 percent of the parts might be fitted wrong in that motorbike you drive. This does not mean that your wheels will fall off when you're cruising on the road. It just means, those wheels belong to a different motorbike which might make it costlier for the manufacturer to make that bike. It also confuses suppliers in their demand forecasts. However, it is mostly for a few products in the starting, and it reaches beyond 95 percent after the product matures in the market.

I interviewed two people in different fields who work in the supply chain field, and their work is specifically related to bills of materials. One of them is in furniture retail and the other one in real estate. While my first friend worked in

---

125. Nell Walker, "Why a Bill of Materials is important," Manufacturing Global (blog), December 14, 2020.

maintaining inventory of exotic furniture items, my other friend worked in repairing and rebuilding properties and selling them off at a good profit. Two very uncommon industries, right? Well, they seemed to have a similar story with their problems and resolution through AI. While you can deal with furniture as physical items and arrange them in a facility at your will, it is way harder to consider a housing project that requires repairs and construction work to prepare it for resale. In any product industry, like furniture, your BOM is limited and depends directly on the suppliers you engage with. AI helped my friend secure a good record of each transaction and create purchase orders (POs) quickly. This automation meant shrinking his daily struggle with documentation to just an hour instead of a whole day. He also used barcodes to arrange his SKUs perfectly.

My other friend was happy about the boom we have in apps. His operations were mostly connecting with contractors and securing the best material from places like Home Depot at lowest prices. Well, why not create a digital channel with your contractors and your potential customers to create transparency? He says, "The more transparent you are with a customer, the better they pay you." His business doesn't have a strict rule about pricing a renovation work. So, if he shows that the work was authentic, he can get paid handsomely.

The Moral of the story is—more the accuracy of BOM, the fewer parts mismatch a product has while undergoing production. For inventory managers, this might dictate how big the safety stock they would need in their stores, based on the performance of the supplier.[126] AI plays the role of a crystal ball to clearly look into the future and anticipates

126. Ibid.

patterns which humans might miss in this whole scenario. This is what enhances effectiveness of Lean processes.

This is just a simple example of what AI can do in the very intrinsic process of a supply chain. Many possibilities exist for processes with the power of data and the capability of AI in thinking and automating on their own. In the arena of procurements and auctions, virtual sourcing is the next milestone. This involves developing a collaborative supply chain structure that rapidly advances e-tender virtual auctions with strategic and preferred supplier groups.

Another example is within forecasting. Advancing forecast demand modeling is a way for predictive and directional market analysis to identify what manufacturing technology you need to meet current or future product designs and anticipated customer needs.[127] This allows blueprinting the digital factory by creating a very transparent view of operations, where minimal human involvement is needed or wanted in very fast and repetitive tasks; this applies to Lean flow, pull, and optimized automation and robotic integration to run lights-out as needed. In essence, AI will design processes extracting Lean principles as needed without human involvement.

Tesla Story

A GE report states that the Industrial Internet will increase US productivity by 1 to 1.5 percentage points which will add ten to fifteen trillion dollars in GDP in the next twenty

---

127. "Demand Forecasting Methods: Using Machine Learning and Predictive Analytics to See the Future of Sales," Altexsoft (blog), November 11, 2019, accessed December 20, 2020.

years. In the next three years, 1.7 million new robots will be installed, one Bain report remarks. It will be more of *cobots*, or collaborative robots, changing the way they are controlled in manufacturing setups.[128]

In my discussion with Mr. Bob Rush, the Lean coach from Tesla, he shared an interesting story about how Tesla went backward on a robot just because of the right suggestions from data that he and his team received at that time. Working since 1980s, he had seen a lot of transformation in technology and trainings coming in from Japan. He mentioned the evolution of coding on the shop floor and simple solutions such as Python logs, where you can build pipelines for projects and people can just type in suggestions. It was easy to track the results and tie them into your accounting system. If you could quantify your results, a lot of waste could be eliminated.

There can be millions of lines of code that can help you make a machine run well, not to mention the number of iterations required, which creates complexity. Not all problems can be solved through code and automation. Bob worked with Hewlett-Packard and learnt one thing from there: it is important to know how critical people are. His focus remained on people, and he carried this even at Tesla.

One of Bob's peers at Tesla came from General Assembly moved into Lean. He was a Toyota guy, so he knew Lean. Bob's boss also approved of his capabilities. One day, they met at one of the cafeterias, and the Toyota guy went, "I got something to show you."

He made Bob go to visit the general assembly which was not far away from their office. It was surprising for Bob to

128. Agence France-Presse, "GE Says 'Industrial Internet' Could be Worth Trillions," Industry Week, November 26, 2012.

stand in front of a huge robot in the middle of the shop floor.

Bob said, "Oh, okay, I have seen robots," and he replies, "Let's just watch it for a little bit and see what happens," and Bob watched patiently.

Within a few minutes, he watched all these people working around but the robot did nothing. So Bob said, "What's the robot there for?" and he goes, "Well, they put the robot in there to do that step but the operators are doing a process that we have discovered the robot cannot do. When they finally got the robot to do it, it took three times more time than the team. So, the manager just stopped using it."

Figure 3: Tesla shopfloor is perceived as a land of robots and automation.

Bob asks, "Okay, well, how long have they been working on it?"

"A year."

"They've been working on it for a year and they can't figure out how to make it work like a human?"

"Okay, well that's bad. That needs to get the attention of Tyson, who was in this area, now that we have a really impressive point on this one."

Tyson was the manager of that area and was quick in his approach to every improvement. Off he went to analyze the process and implement the change with his team. They eliminated the robot. They moved it to his excess stock room where people put things that didn't use anymore. It was like a storeroom there and you could then use the robot for anything.

Bob told Tyson, "If anybody in your area claims that robot, I want to know it because I want to know what to do with it." They had a good laugh, and Bob told him, "You are a God of Lean, my friend. Because you eliminated a robot at Tesla."

I have seen people eliminate robots before, but not at Tesla. That's a good example where you realize the power of process over technology, and these are the kinds of stories that I'm fascinated by, too. Tesla seems to be a company that is highly automated, and they really want to go toward a completely automated approach.

We see inefficiencies, so we decide to just buy more robots and do the same process. We think that will help us get the number we need. But we never increase the yield that much. That's a major gap that needs to be addressed today. What does this say about Lean coexisting with the ever-evolving Industry 4.0? The Industry 4.0 paradigm centers on deploying advanced technology to develop integrated and highly adaptive manufacturing systems and supply chains. Lean follows a paradigm surrounded by people, processes, and a culture of continuous improvement leading to breakthrough productivity levels. At first glance, Lean may sound like much more people-centric and anti-technology owing to its focus on processes and management. People and process aspects, which are central to Lean, will still play a critical role even for the most advanced systems in the future and would still require a human component to them.[129]

That is, unless we are talking about AI being so advanced that it takes decision-making into its own hands. For example, in critical industries like finance, investments run on high-stakes decisions. Here, a huge discussion is replacing the experts in their suits and ties guiding you through an investment scheme with AI advisors guiding you through an app in the same way. It calls into question the ethics and accuracy of decisions that an AI might achieve. That is a topic of business ethics and deserves a whole separate book. Lean works on removing those biases on the people level. It roughs up the edges by creating a practical experience around processes. Hence, it can be safely assumed that for the next twenty-five to thirty years, Lean methodology is going to co-exist with AI.

---

129. Ibid.

CHAPTER 11

CONFLUENCE OF THE FUTURE OF MANUFACTURING | LEAN AND AGILE

You can hear a Lean factory.

In the first chapter, we learned about the origin of Lean. It started as a way to streamline the way cars were produced with the same set of actions in the most efficient manner. Lean and Agile are very often used as interchangeable terms by managers who use both of them. What are some similarities? Both Lean and Agile are end-user-focused philosophies used to develop high quality products using fewer resources. Agile is an iterative process, as is Lean with its continuous improvement. Having a clear understanding between the two is important today since it leads to a short-term and temporary implementation if the team is not sure about its selection.

I was lured into coercing my manager to abandon the sequential way of managing projects ("waterfall") and shift to Agile at my production plant, but I didn't know if it was actually feasible. Let's see how they compare.

Traditional Lean vs Traditional Agile

Every time a project kicks off, three metrics are always under play: cost of production, time to delivery, and man-hours involved.

The cost of production is nothing, but the total cost of raw materials, manpower, and equipment resources used to make up the product. That involves all the *Muda* types that are present in the process (remember TIMWOOD?) at every step. So, if I am trying to have fewer defects, I will avoid the resource wastage in replacing it with a new product for the same customer. Similarly, man-hours are nothing, but the total number of hours employed by a worker in creating the product. We also talk about the level of skill associated with the worker. Actually, employer skills have become another asset for the company to gain future growth.

Agile intersects Lean mostly in the second metric, time to delivery. Agile is fail-fast. It involves working and then building on top of it—less planning, more work. Also, Agile is mostly centered around "building" something. For example, this might be a physical product or a software or simply an HR system to be implemented widely around the company. This means that in Agile, you don't care to build the complete product all at once. You start with a minimum viable model, test it on a lower scale, and grow it as it succeeds and gets more impactful. As I briefly mentioned in an earlier chapter about the origin of Agile, it was started to standardize the amount of work done among the programmers to launch a new application faster. In the 1980s, programmers were struggling to release one product, taking months to years developing it only to find that it became obsolete by the time it hit the market.[130] Their mistake was developing software on a virtual conveyor belt. They used the waterfall technique, which involves doing all the tasks in a sequence of A-B-C and so on. They could not start step B until step A was completed.[131]

The new Agile method replaced this to smaller chunks of iterations. The product was broken down into basic features, and product version "one" would be made in a week and then tested for its minimum viability.[132] Iteration "two" would involve adding more features to it and testing again. Based on customer feedback, the product would be improved more accurately and quickly.

Imagine that you want to build a car. If you start from scratch, you'll definitely take months building it. If the basic motive for you is to reach from destination A to destination B, you can start with the basic things that you need: wheels, seat, and a handle. You work on combining these basic attributes, test it for stability, speed, strength of material, etc., and convert those materials into a bicycle. Now, you want to add more speed, better performance, and stronger materials. You take more such feedback from your bicycle customers, add some more effort, and add a motor to it to get a motorbike. When you are confident enough and have developed the product at

130. Thorbjørn Sigberg, "Lean vs Agile vs Lean-Agile," *Medium* (blog), March 8, 2019.
131. Jose Maria Delos Santos, "Agile vs. Waterfall: Differences in Software Development Methodologies?," Project Management, August 20, 2020.
132. "Agile vs Lean,'" Planview, accessed February 21, 2021.

a stage where you can play with more components and attributes, you put in that effort and develop a car! At every stage, you had a functional product and added more features as you improved your previous version of the "car." That's Agile.

Time to delivery is, generally, the first metric used to measure the "agility" of a software developer team. Lean follows a similar target of faster delivery to the customers. However, Lean focuses on process rather than working in batch sizes to get a product. Lean teams put customers first by focusing on building and improving processes that allow them to eliminate waste (by the Lean definition). Basically, if a customer wouldn't pay for it, it's a waste. Too much work in progress and the manual completion of a task (when it can be automated) are both considered waste in Lean thinking.[133]

Another difference is on the focus of a product at hand. Lean applies to repetitive processes aiming to produce a new (and identical) product each time. Agile applies to repetitive processes where we iterate on improving *one* product. So, in our bicycle to car example, with Lean, if we are making one thousand cars and they all stick to their quality requirements, they will have minimum wastes and will be identical to each other. On the other hand, Agile is a step before that and involves building that first car from the basic version of the bicycle.

Similar to Lean implementations, Agile has its own challenges. I'm a fan of how Amazon is always customer-focused in every sphere of its business. I had to see if they apply Agile. In a conversation with one of the senior software engineers at Amazon, I got to know that the teams err on the side of the customer. They have to think out of the box to deliver faster. Everything

---

133. Ibid.

depends on the output that you want to get from your project. The metrics in focus are time to market, cost to build, cost to maintain, and cost to extend it. The team front-loads that cost in terms of manpower, thinking whether a designer working on a short-term solution could work for one month now vs the cost they would bear to plan six months' worth of maintenance and repair of the code later. This short-term plug-in solution is called "throwaway" work. This code or design may take one week to build but is not horizontally copy-able.

This interpretation for Agile has also evolved for other fields like healthcare. We think of an app associated with every personal health service that we avail today. Tom Miller, CIO of Anthem, explains it below:

> *"In Agile, you aim for a minimum viable product. That forces thinking around what's the highest priority, what delivers the most value, what's a definable piece of functionality or capability that can be implemented to do some good... In healthcare, traditionally, the value was in processing claims. But now there are thousands of little interactions that bring value to consumers every day, whether that's through a health tracker or a fitness app or something else in the digital world."*[34]
>
> —TOM MILLER, ANTHEM CIO

Another challenge for Agile is change to resistance and adapting to those changes. This one is similar to Lean and drains out most resources for completing an existing project.

---

134. Carla Rudder, "Anthem CIO: How agile helped us drive value," *The Enterprisers Project*, February 26, 2018.

Agile also faces a lot of communication struggles, since the teams need to be on the same page at every product stage and at every step of the work.[135]

S&OP: Sales Team vs Operations Team

An example of how Lean and Agile come together can be seen through a rather non-traditional application in supply chain. One of the biggest tasks of a supply chain is determining a forecast, also known as sales and operations planning. To put it in the perspective of one of my interviewees, it is a tug of war between the sales team and operations team. Sales thrives on serving the customers as quickly as possible. They want real-time data for everything. You ask the sales team to give you a sales forecast, and they will come up with extrapolated versions of the current demand. Most of the time, this picture is highly optimistic and beyond the capacity of the operations team. I have witnessed this firsthand while working on quarterly production forecast of trucks at Tata. The sales team remained so optimistic that they would ask us to double our production in three months. They prefer to think of the present and want their projections to be "live."

However, it would be a huge mistake for operations to work with such numbers. Operations and manufacturing folks are more concerned about the future. They have to plan their capacity according to the production plan. This includes manpower, shifts, equipment, and material resources, to name a few. And so, they need to have a steady forecast of

---

135. Lena Boiser, "What is Lean Agile Project Management?" Kanban Zone, April 21, 2020.

the next twelve to twenty-four months, which gives them an indication of how much manpower and equipment they need to work with for achieving that plan. They cannot work with a highly variable dataset that the sales team provides them. They love to work in teams and ensure a Lean process *after* the plan is set. That is why companies do S&OP meetings every month or twice a month—to strike a balance between the two teams and make their projections more reliable.[136]

A current standard in the industry is to look at the past two or three years of patterns and build a projection out of it. But the whole process is so manual that it takes at least a dozen meetings to finalize the numbers. With automated forecast solutions, it can be done relatively quickly. This process is an example where Lean can be applied.

I wouldn't be able to give a blanket solution for all the S&OP meetings out there but there are a couple things worth mentioning that worked for a couple of my interviewees: centralization of data and integration of teams. They call it Lean S&OP. Think about the wastes generated in the whole process—data is key to the final decision-making and it tends to get passed around so many times that it wastes time and resources. This lengthy communication can be truncated if all that information is quickly available to you at one place. Solutions like Box folders and Microsoft Teams are trying to implement it today. Creating a central platform eliminates the need to email an updated file every day. Integration of finance, sales, and operations teams is another Lean solution.

And think how it triggers the growth ahead. If you create a manufacturing environment where material flows

---

136. Henry Canitz, "Lean Principles and Sales & Operations Planning (S&OP)," Logility, accessed February 21, 2020.

with minimum waste, but you can't predict capacity and material-availability issues in time to mitigate them, you will revert to firefighting and finger-pointing. Even if you do an excellent job of future planning, poor material flows will result in higher inventory levels, longer lead times, and lower profitability.

Lean x Agile =?

> *There is great synergy between Agile and Lean. The irony is that one is based on the other, but once you start becoming more Agile, you will become leaner more easily.*
>
> —NIGEL THURLOW, CHIEF OF AGILE, TOYOTA

What would Lean x Agile mean? Can they co-exist? Absolutely! In my discussion with an Agile coach, he showed his praise for how industries are realizing the importance of Agile methodology in product development. I also came across a great saying from Lean-Agile coach Thorbjorn Sigberg, who says, *"Lean principles are equally relevant in Agile contexts like software development. Improving lead time still makes sense. Deferring commitment still makes sense. Reducing defects and waste still makes sense. Reducing variability (often) makes sense."*[137]

While Lean strives to improve the process that delivers a product, Agile strives to improve the product itself. For

---

137. Thorbjorn Sigberg, "Lean vs Agile vs Lean-Agile," *Medium* (blog), March 8, 2019.

companies thinking to roll out multiple new products, they need Agile to save time on their "time to market" or "lead time to launch." Once they achieve it, manufacturing takes care of using Lean principles to get the best process to make a million copies of that product. The nice thing about Lean and Agile is that a great synergy exists between the two. The irony is that one is based on the other, but once you start becoming more Agile, you will become leaner more easily. Once you set up the team to bring agility in their work, the same *Kaizens* start happening faster. On the other hand, if you have a streamlined process, the team engages in meaningful communication, and iterations on products become faster and more successful.

CIOs who are succeeding with digital transformation have their own definitions of "Agile." For Zack Hicks, chief digital officer and CIO of Toyota North America and CEO of Toyota Connected, Agile is about "delivering only what the customer asks and no more a minimally viable product, or MVP, then hearing what customers like or don't like and building that into the next iteration of the product."[138]

At Comcast, Rick Rioboli, EVP and CIO, has a vast technology ecosystem at his disposal. His team includes product teams and technology teams, and he draws insights and offers counsel to three different technology innovation labs of sorts: an incubator called LIFT Labs, Comcast Ventures, and Comcast Labs.[139] While discussing the application of clean data and managing powerful language processing in service assistance for Comcast, he stressed on something that relates

138. Carla Rudder, "Agile is Ready for its Next Big Break, CIOs Say," *The Enterprisers Project*, August 23, 2018.
139. Peter High, "Comcast CIO Rick Rioboli Sits at the Center of an Innovation Ecosystem," *Forbes,* October 7, 2019.

directly with the way Agile operates: "To create a culture of innovation, we had to stop taking the orders and think less like renters and more like owners. Why run fifteen different projects around a sales platform? Why not build one reusable set of capabilities... We became more innovative when we started to build new solutions on reusable layers."[140]

Carolyn Lum, senior vice president and head of Continuous Improvement and Philips Excellence, explains how they implemented Lean thinking in the business: "Until a few years ago, Philips' Lean improvement work focused primarily on manufacturing—with some of our factories having been on a Lean journey for decades. We knew that in order to unlock the full potential of Lean, we needed to go beyond manufacturing." Phillips deploys Lean thinking holistically and values the early adopters in this area.[141]

Carolyn believes that the end-to-end processes that serve customers touch every bit of Philips, so everybody needs to join the journey. This is true of any value chain that you can imagine. To make your transitions seamless, you need to tell everyone about Lean, involve everyone, and think holistically. Another mantra for her has been vocalizing local successes globally. Communicating quick wins helps people to adopt best practices quickly and get a morale boost for the person who did it.

On the other hand, Jeroen Tas, the CIO and chief strategy officer at Phillips, believes in the power of Agile and Lean to make everyday trade-offs in the teams and prioritize business-critical decisions. Phillips has grown into multiple

140. Martha Heller, "How Comcast IT moved from order-taker to innovator," *CIO,* December 2, 2020.

141. Carolyn Lum, Jakob Brix Danielsen, "Lean Transformation: Eight Tips from Philips," Planet Lean, November 7, 2019.

products and requires Agile in constantly evolving in its product design.[142]

The concept of business agility goes beyond skill set. Most businesses have functional silos between the business and the central IT teams, and they are not set up to be Agile organizations. Isaac Sacolick, author of *Driving Digital* and a former CTO, also believes in the cultural change that unites Agile and Lean. He too stresses on the need of the end-to-end projects woven together. He goes, "[It] requires experimentation and change management, requires us to take feedback during the project... We've got to get teams to think together, that takes an Agile way of operating. That means collaborative teams, measuring input and output of short cycles. It means being able to show progress and response every couple of weeks. It takes Business and IT people working together—that's why I call it enterprise agility. We talk about scaling it globally, it's not just working in one location."[143]

As digital transformation progresses, we must focus on knowledge sharing more than the materials or the people in the team. It is how we manage the information that is going to determine our speed of work and quality of results.

---

142. Jeroen Tas, "Agile, Lean and the Art of Business—IT Integration," i-CIO, March 2014.

143. "How CIOs can Enable an Agile Organization", Bizagi, September 12, 2018.

PART 4

CHAPTER 12

LEAN OF THE FUTURE | HYBRID LEAN

———

It's my goal to transition Toyota from an automobile company to a mobility company, and the possibilities of what we can build, in my mind, are endless."
—AKIO TOYODA, PRESIDENT, TOYOTA[144]

The moment the ball dropped at Times Square on January 1st, 2020, we entered a new decade. A decade that promised efficiency and speed through technology. One of the best quotes that I came across describing this new decade is: *"It's no longer the Big beating the Small, but the Fast beating the Slow."*—Eric Pearson (CIO, International Hotel Group)[145]

———

144. Dave West, Nigel Thurlow, "Agile Transformation—The Success Story of Scrum & Toyota" (Interview, Agile for Automotive Summit, Detroit, MI, May 17, 2019).

145. Kintone, "11 Digital Transformation Quotes to Lead Change and Inspire Action," *Medium* (blog), May 6, 2019.

Ford was the first company in US to transition from a "manual" mode to "machine" mode. By automating the lines for mass production, it created a pathway for companies to treat manpower as a part of machine power. For decades, organizations that embraced the scientific management and modern technology adoption quickly managed to dominate their markets; the twentieth century can thus also be called the "management century."[146]

The mantra for the future of companies and future entrepreneurs is: "Disrupt your future or find new opportunities." Almost everything in terms of success is governed by how well you understand the market and disrupt your field of expertise to lure the customers before others. In a gradual course of things, there will be new opportunities created with new technology trends but, as history holds, small companies have an edge over mature companies in being nimble and Agile. They can change the course quicker than large corporations.[147]

The 1980s and '90s

Through the 1980s and '90s, people weren't always hired for their brains. There was a lot of "I pay you to do what I say" rather than "I pay you to think." That has been the biggest change, even in non-Lean companies. You can see that people now want to be heard. One example is the exit interview that you give when you leave a company. At present, it is meant to relieve an employee by giving full feedback to him and

---

146. Christopher Null, "10 Companies Killing it at Scaling Agile," Techbeacon, October 15, 2020, Accessed February 8 2021.
147. Customer Insight, "What is 360 Degree Feedback?," Accessed October 31 2020.

taking his feedback for the company. The company and the HR want to know what the exiting employee thought about the company and how his team and his seniors performed, and this involves a 360-degree feedback for his performance as well. In short, a listening process takes place. In old days, they didn't really care. The HR wanted you to give a points rating, maybe from a scale of 1 to 10, and other basic formalities in those exit interviews. Now, those interviews are intense, as they think about the treatment of people and much more. This is what's really evolved with the use of data and tech.[148]

In terms of technology on the manufacturing shopfloor, when I interact with multiple senior leaders, they mention that they never saw computers on the production shop floor at all. They started with CNC machines or mechanical equipment that provided some digital reading on a black and white screen but nothing more. The people on the floor didn't interact with computers at all—they were treated like dummies. People who were trained by old Japanese guys carried old habits, such as carrying a notebook and writing notes by hand. My earlier boss followed the same habits. He was *good*—never missed anything and kept records of his notes ready. If he needed, he could backtrack his notes to refer from a five-year-old stand-up meeting that no one else would ever remember. I, on the other hand, use my sticky notes that had a short life of maximum of a week or two. I carried my laptop to the shop whenever I got a chance, depending mostly on it for any discussion with my colleagues about a project. From the perspective of manufacturing professionals of the '80s, we're doing things on the computer that they wouldn't have ever dreamed of.

---

148. Ibid.

And then there's data management on the factory floor. We can get data so quickly now. I still want people to go to the factory floor and do some time studies, but it's more to get a sense of line balance meant for the actual data, because humans can't analyze data as quickly as computers. So, it becomes more efficient to take some extrapolated data from the computer. The data we use is still an average, but most of the time it is more accurate than the data before.

Another manufacturing professional from a leading FMCG company from the 1980s that I interviewed takes pride in how he used numbers to guide his decisions. He goes, "I know what I need to do to figure out where the deviations are right, and I highlight a little number. The moment I see that small number, which tends to be an outlier, I ask questions like, "Is this a data entry mistake or do you have somebody on your floor that knows a way of doing things that nobody else does?" And what I find is about 70 percent of the time it's actually somebody doing something different than anybody else. In the old days, they would tell you to follow the rules. It was never a part of standard work."

Such changes require an upgrade to Lean practices, whether it is the change of analysis tools, the thought process of people on the shop floor, the change of equipment from CNC machines to robotic automation, or simply the type of people changing from baby boomers to millennials. What revolutions await Lean manufacturing?

A New Revolution

Lean, as a tool, has helped in such scenarios to help large corporations pivot this change. In earlier chapters, we talked about process management, starting at the shop floor, and then evolving into Lean management to control manpower as well. While we may lament the long time that it has taken organizations to understand Lean as a progressive system of management practice, it shows that our perception and understanding of Lean evolves over time. This reflects the learning that occurred as people gained firsthand experience with Lean and exposure to the work of other practitioners and thought leaders.

A couple things are influencing this evolution: current changes in tech and the way we interact in work-teams. The way we work is defined by the way we share information. The next step to utilize Lean is to optimize our information sharing systems across teams. I discussed this briefly earlier while comparing Lean with Agile. Whether it is a service-intensive workplace where you collaborate with teams across departments or a product-building meeting, information plays a key role in keeping everyone on the same page. I have seen multiple companies spend on specific program managers who have a single deliverable to drive the projects and communicate with everyone to keep the information sharing smooth. Even product managers have a huge role of information management while launching a test run or piloting a new product that they are building. The 'knowledge workers' are stuck to their screens for over 1,700 hours a year, just to coordinate the projects.[149]

Another part of the changes in tech involve the use of data to get us the right decisions. We have shifted from predominantly reactive to now mostly proactive projects. Since every

---

149. Grant Bailey, "Office workers spend 1,700 hours a year in front of a computer screen," *Independent*, July 23, 2018.

industry now has at least a thirty years' worth of knowledge and experience, they lean on their past to not repeat their mistakes. Even regression needs thirty data points to give high-confidence results! The array of data collecting and processing solutions which we discussed in the data chapter is another protective layer for Lean projects. And the layer gets stronger with our progress in AI and ML.

The second revolution is our team interaction. Millennials have witnessed their own fair share of market catastrophes, which have made them resilient, smarter, and faster. Be it the dot-com bubble, the 2009 depression, or the most recent COVID pandemic, every decade becomes a learning curve and transforms the way teams work. A lot of well-established systems were rattled by COVID in 2020 and it has already posed challenge for many companies in terms of working from home. Remote working is helpful only for a limited number of industries, and the rest have to figure out a balance between managing their physical workshops by keeping people six feet apart and sending people home to control a portion of work from there. Future business trends in 2020 look to dominate the technology segment with unlimited innovation and the adoption of data-driven technologies.

Evolution of Lean Concepts

Derek Leong, a Lean manager at Tesla, believes in a linear evolution of the concepts. "Data is centric to Lean's evolution in near future. With advances in technology, data availability and analysis will naturally help to highlight sources of waste. Whereas Lean currently is often associated with 'learning to see,' it will need to become much more heavily focused on 'learning to innovate.'" As more and more waste is squeezed out of a system, one can either:

1. Fundamentally rethink the way things are being done, admit that their 'no waste system' is still actually full of waste they never realized, and create a new way of functioning.
2. Find new and creative ways to increase the amount of value that they are able to provide.

It is fascinating how many diverse perspectives can be built around one concept. For me, there is another line of thought about people who would be working on these concepts. It is a huge shift from traditional Japanese *Sensei* to current Gen Y culture.

AI Replacing Lean Coaches

A very likely trajectory for Lean is to replace the Lean coaches of today with AI assistants. At present, a lot of companies employ Lean coaches who have been originally trained by the Japanese *Sensei*. Gary Weber and Bob Rush are seasoned Lean consultants who have worked for every industry from Tesla in automotive to Boeing in airlines, and all tier-1 and tier-2 suppliers in between. Gary mentioned in one of our discussions that he doesn't see anything replacing the tool of visual management. There is no other software that can actually alarm you for overproduction or a wrong process than a simple red light over a machine. He says, "Lean implementation is not necessarily cookie-cutter. And AI will help it become more standardized. But I really stress on it to be useless if it is not visual. That to me is a big challenge. It can be very complex to code and maintain a database, but it can't be complex to the end user. It's got to be graphic and binary yes-no answers at a glance."

One thing that will change with the future is the role of different stakeholders. You have managers for everything. A warehouse manager controls inventory and associates. A shift manager works to make decisions every day to make sure that you achieve the production target. A demand planner takes care of multiple factors to share a forecast with sales and marketing team.[150] But AI is going to be a step further in helping these areas. The quantification and risk measurement of the future decisions might become faster with AI. For Lean, everything starts and ends with the customer. It is the duty of the Lean leader to guide their customer to a simple vision for the future.[151]

If they want technology, they should be informed of the various tech options that they have as *tools* for their operations improvement. Bob, who has been a *Sensei* for his team at Tesla, had similar thoughts. He views AI and IoT as providing an integrated smart guidance to anyone on the shop floor, which the coaches provide today. Those systems would partner with you to help you take informed decisions. They would teach you to use correct principles of Lean when you face a roadblock. They would help define and choose your battles wisely for you, but they can never replace a human.

---

150. "What to Know About in Lean Warehouse Management," Industrial Distribution, January 4, 2017.

151. Bill Stevens, "The Future of Lean: Four Disruptors of the Decade," *Lean Construction Blog* (blog), July 2, 2019.

Generation Next

A great change that accompanies this trend in AI assistants is "Generation Next." In the next ten years, the workforce will be filled with Generation Y and Z.[152] Millennials are more likely to explore new skills and opportunities. Whereas previous generations tended to be more risk averse, millennials enjoy taking risks and adopting new ideas—all of which are important traits for driving supply chain and manufacturing innovation.[153] They function very differently than their former counterparts. Lean, as a concept, was transferred to the US by Japanese *Sensei*. Right now, what we have, at least in the manufacturing industry, are top students of those Japanese teachers who have dedicated their life spreading those teachings far and wide in the North American continent. They are the second-generation Lean teachers. What will the next generation of teachers look like? I have a number of friends who, like me, are fascinated by the concepts but get fewer chances to practice them due to technological disruptions. This is what brings us to the AI teachers. Technology could be the future of coaches.

Lean coaches just share their experience with a team, while AI enhances this experiential learning. Most of the things that a Lean coach does is understanding their client and personalizing the solutions for the given problem.[154] AI will have to be more universal at the base before getting

---

152. Steve Minter, "Will Millennials Change Manufacturing?," Industry Week, December 28, 2017.
153. Brett Christie, "Generation Z's Impact on the Future of Work," Worldatwork, May 31, 2019.
154. Gerd Aulinger, Mike Rother, "The Role of the Lean Coach," November 2012.

personalized like the human coaches. So, one challenge that remains for AI is: how do you make an AI software package that is universal to factories worldwide? Hopefully, not tailored to a factory but something every factory can use. Forget workers—the system still has to be backflush. The need for work orders doesn't need to be there anymore because the "information conduits" through the whole system back flush everything. And it's a pull system that replenishes the inventory, not a push system. Lean accepts a pull system; hence, this aligns the whole drill.[155]

The Dark Factory

Have you ever heard of a dark factory? The manufacturing community is fascinated about the possibility of a scenario where everything gets fully automated. This would mean we could just put all the raw material at one end, not care about what happens in the box in the middle, and just drive away with output on the other end. The box in the middle is a lights-out facility with an army of robots and AI thinkers that can make all the quality decisions for the products for a human being.[156]

One of my interviewees is fascinated with the dark factory concept. He mentioned it in our interview, saying, "I'm thinking of things like lights out manufacturing, where you just have a warehouse full of robots completely dark or truck shows up at the facility and the shutter closes, and the warehouse of robots are working. With visual inspection

---

155. Dr. Manu Melwin Roy, "Lean Leadership," ResearchGate, April 2019.
156. Justus Krüger, "Will Industry 4.0 Create a Dark Factory?," *Metrology News*, March 7, 2019.

happening with IR cameras, takt-time controllers for pneumatic control and other forms of IoT to control the machines already exists for the dark factory to work today. This is not even like I'm talking about something out of *Black Mirror.*"

The manufacturing world is divided on this thought, though. Many complications can happen beyond one's expectations. We need to be absolutely sure of all the possible risks and mitigation steps needed to cover those risks if we think about a dark factory and want to abandon the manufacturing plants altogether. But, hey, that is what future looks like! This might be a utopian vision for Lean processes where, at least in the production field, the discussion will shift from noting down movements of people to the selection of the most efficient machines and taking a thirty-thousand-foot view of the value chain.

Hybrid Lean

Digital Lean is not a new set of Lean principles, but it enhances the principles to make their application more powerful. While systems of record, such as enterprise resource planning, often report on operations as they impact company and plant financials, many digital Lean systems of innovation produce detailed information on *all* aspects of a process. Digital Lean uses Industry 4.0 and other digital tools to provide more accurate, precise, and timely information about operations. It not only helps realize Lean principles but also increases the impact of core Lean tools, such as *Kanban*.

Digital Lean also provides an opportunity to target *hidden* components of waste, such as information asymmetry, that often goes unnoticed and cumulatively adds up to higher support costs and reduced efficiency, resulting in tangible bottom-line impact.

Hybrid Lean, on the other hand, has most researchers defining it as the hybrid of Lean and Agile. As we discussed in the chapters earlier, Lean and Agile can co-exist and can in many ways be applied together. Unlike digital Lean, hybrid Lean is more specific to the operational processes influenced by Agile. This means that when a product is still in its initial stages, product design and process design can go hand-in-hand if we achieve a highly efficient feedback loop. There have been studies to implement a hybridized version of Lean for industries. A notable mention is a hybrid Lean-Agile system for the automotive industry that I found. It provides a view of merging technical pillars of Lean and Agile with the help of digital tools of e-manufacturing, electronic value chain, and enterprise resource planning.

Table 1. The technical facet of the hybrid Lean-Agile manufacturing system in terms of Lean and Agile aspects.[157]

	Manufacturing system aspects	
	Lean aspect	**Agile aspect**
Technical pillar of the hybrid Lean-Agile manufacturing system	Flexible focused factories	Innovative value chain strategies
	Fractal e-manufacturing	Designing dynamic manufacturing strategies

---

157. Salah A.M. Elmoselhy, *Hybrid lean-agile manufacturing system technical facet, in automotive sector*, Journal of Manufacturing Systems, Volume 32, Issue 4, 2013, Pages 598-619.

Some of the aspects of a proposed hybrid Lean manufacturing include e-manufacturing, electronic value chain and a modified ERP.

E-Manufacturing: The e-manufacturing architecture has two dimensions. One dimension is internal and comes from the product level, represented by the modular or integral architecture. It has either a standardized interface or a more complex relationship of parts and functions within the manufacturing system. The other dimension is external and deals with the relation among corporations. The hybrid Lean proposes to focus on internal dimension and adopt hybrid modular-integral architecture at the product level. In this hybrid modular-integral architecture, the design constraints are fixed, and the product is distributed to smaller parts. These parts are designed to achieve their maximum performance considering the standardized interface. The hybrid Lean also prefers multiple manufacturing facilities located closely together. It means having all suppliers and aggregate manufacturers located domestically. Although not easily achieved in reality, this manufacturing configuration helps both cost-effectiveness and availability in operations.[158]

Electronic Value Chain: Electronic value chain is another way of digitization of the supply chain. Examples include, leveraging existing radio frequency identification (RFID) and the intranet. A proposed electronic value chain concept can convey real-time data about individual items as they move through the value chain.[159]

Outward-Facing ERP with Private Trade Exchange: An ERP system provides integration between all internal business

---

158. Ibid.

159. Megan Ray Nichols, "RFID and Lean Manufacturing Are a Perfect Pair," Manufacturing, March 12, 2018.

aspects of an enterprise. It would be better if this ERP system was outward facing to extend communication with customers and suppliers. The outward-facing ERP based on PTX (Private Trade Exchange) provides integration between all internal business aspects of an enterprise along with providing an online collaboration model that brings manufacturers, distributors, and customers together to execute trading transactions and to share information about demand, production, availability, and more. The outward-facing ERP based on PTX can increase the efficiency of the value chain and reduce costs to participants.[160]

The proposed manufacturing system hybridizes the technical attributes of both the Lean and Agile manufacturing systems that are in practice. Automakers that have success in the manufacturing business realize the flexibility of:

1. production equipment,
2. chaining plants, and
3. execution of a production order

They are able to increase responsiveness to varying customer needs if they achieve this hybrid Lean in their system successfully. Obviously, the way to this utopian vision is a long and arduous one starting from assessing your current status of Lean or Agile growth and identifying those gaps that can merge them together. This is one of the many possibilities, really, but a plausible one that can be copied by industries other than automotive too.

---

160. Salah A.M. Elmoselhy, *Hybrid lean-agile manufacturing system technical facet, in automotive sector*, Journal of Manufacturing Systems, Volume 32, Issue 4, 2013, Pages 598-619.

CHAPTER 13

SEVEN WAYS LEAN
CAN EVOLVE

The title of this chapter was inspired by the fact that I like reading articles with titles like "Eight Things to Consider When You Travel" or "Twelve Facts That Will Blow Your Mind" (although at some point, it becomes too much when I get bombarded with them in my inbox—thanks AI!). Why not collate everything that applies to the evolution of Lean in seven major bullets?

We exist in a very interesting moment in history. Just like the 1950s when radio transitioned to televisions, in the 2020s the smart phone is the new television and TV is the new radio.[161] In a factory, diagnostic applications and RPA are the new *robots*. So far, we have discussed the impact of software on operational processes of the products. We've touched upon the challenges Lean possesses, differences between Lean and Agile, digital and physical products, and

---

161. "Golden Age of Radio in the US," Digital Public Library of America, accessed Oct 6, 2020.

how leaders consider data sacred. The future of Lean could be hybrid Lean or digital Lean. In my short four-year exploration, I could see multiple paths to follow and a variety of trends that could lead to an evolved Lean philosophy, but I've chosen to be patient. After all, so many industries are still in the initial stages of their Lean development and they need to jump a few years ahead to catch up with the digital developments. This chapter condenses a few of those trends for my readers to ponder upon as a way to revisit some of the discussions we've had so far.

I did a survey with eight of my favorite podcasts on NPR and Spotify that talk about manufacturing and the idea of technological innovations. They were unanimous on one thing: Lean of the future is more intrinsic for companies than outsiders think. Every company has their own internal consulting teams. Those teams are more knowledgeable and smarter about their work than ever before. Every company has their own arsenal of "continuous improvement champions" who can be trained and used to improve the bottom line. Eventually, Lean of the future has a possibility to be on auto-pilot and be a strong backbone to the analytics team looking to optimize on the go. Nevertheless, let's look at the seven trends.

1. *Go with the wind—"digital Lean"*

I remember keeping my first phone for four years before shifting to a new one, but my last phone lasted just fifteen months. This was not because it went bad—I sold it to buy an upgraded version, which launched this year. The same happens in the process space too. Robotic process automation, or RPA, is jargon one used to hear in 2015. RPA was the answer to all the worries and demands of a frustrated manufacturer, but

IoT and Blockchain soon took over.[162] They became the new fad and industry immediately shifted toward it. If companies don't invest in these trends quick enough, they slowly build up a backlog for their digital advancement. One million dollars invested today can help them save five million tomorrow. If they don't spend it today, they spend the same amount first on the consultant who takes three months to discover that gap and then another couple million dollars to develop capability. They essentially start playing catch-up with technology if they don't act fast enough. A vicious cycle, so to speak.

A year ago, I interviewed for a tech strategy firm in Washington, DC, where I met really insightful people. They specialize in strategy and implementation of IT-based solutions for a range of industries. In one of my interactions with a senior manager there, he gave me a really good example of how the digital transformation evolves in a company. He explains it in three major steps: "The first time a company might call themselves digital or 'digitally transformed' is when they are actually just making sure that their data is not stored on paper, but into the PCs or laptops." Most of the companies are still at this stage. This conversion is called *digitization*, and this is the first step toward digital transformation. "The second step is *digitalization*, the use of digital technologies and digitized data to impact how work gets done, transform how customers and companies engage and interact, and create new (digital) revenue streams. Digitalization helps the company to ditch the physical meetings and collaborate online. Ditch the manual file sharing and centralize resources on a cloud. The third and most advanced

---

162. Narender Thota, "The Rise of RPA in the Manufacturing Industry," VentureIQ, October 16, 2020.

stage is *digital transformation*. It involves people using sensors and remote equipment, which is responsible for recording the data for analysis. It creates an ecosystem of big data driven decision-making and preemptive tasks distributed seamlessly among the team. Everything is a symphony of relevant information flowing across the company where it is needed the most."

Blockchain is another development that has enabled the companies to secure their information while sharing it externally. The system runs independently most of the time. Consider a supply chain of coffee production. Blockchain gives a tremendous end-to-end feedback loop from the farmer to the coffee cup you're drinking. It might help a farmer in Brazil keeping track of a coffee packet being sold in Washington, DC, by providing him with an update of how much the customer liked it. The farmer can, in turn, improve upon his produce. Starbucks did it in a partnership with Microsoft.[163] The most attractive attribute of this is zero human intervention.

The conversation with the tech consultants gave me the impression that right now, Industry 4.0 is limited in the manufacturing field in real application. I got a chance to see this form of digital advancement at Amazon. Not long ago, associates had to walk more than ten miles every day to locate products from the shelves, pick them, and send them for packing. The packer would walk to keep it in specific rows and columns of racks in the warehouse. Now, they have effortless robots that can be summoned right next to the associate by scanning the product's barcode and all of that walking is removed. We saw the Kroger example from before,

---

163. Lucas Mearian, "From coffee bean to cup: Starbucks brews a block-chain-based supply chain with Microsoft," *Computer World*, May 7, 2019.

where they use RPA to take care of all the repetitive steps of scanning, picking, and stowing to increase operations speed.[164] What I saw in the Amazon fulfillment center was the epitome of speed and accuracy made possible by an army of scanners, sensors, and smart roller conveyors, which otherwise would take hours of manual labor to match. Although I didn't see anything fly around at Amazon, who knows—maybe the next step in automation is to use the space close to the roof and evolve the current stowing system.[165] Maybe that's the drones!

2. *More skilled workers, more uniform implementation*

The industries are concerned about the future of work. For developing countries, it is the speed of growth on "unicorn start-ups" more so than many of the developed nations. To give a perspective, in early 2020, there were over two hundred companies in China, more than twenty in India, and ten in Israel, all of these coming in top seven countries with unicorn start-ups.[166] On the other end of this spectrum, global trends such as globalization, demographic shifts, climate change, and technology have already brought profound shifts to the world of work for labor markets of the world. For developed countries, the change is in diversification of the workforce and developing remote learning.

164. Vipul Parekh, "Integration of RPA with Blockchain—A Potential New Way to Re-Think Business Models," LinkedIn (blog), March 20, 2019.
165. Maria Halkias, "Kroger's new robotic warehouse can fill a 50-item order in less than 10 minutes," *The Dallas Morning News*, September 12, 2019.
166. Jennifer Rudden, "Number of unicorns worldwide as of January 2020, by country," Statista, December 7, 2020.

There is an interesting situation with countries where they have forty million workers unemployed and companies still lament about a dearth of employees with the relevant skills they need.[167] In between the pandemic and changing virtual tech, we have learned to use our skills while working from home. However, this is just for skilled workers and maybe for bachelors and creatives—not for everyone. Experts have their own concerns about what will happen to low-skilled jobs once the robots take over. This is something that needs to be broken down into real facts. When I say manual or low-skilled jobs, I mean work that involves repeated work that a robot can learn and do effortlessly compared to a human. In turn, it immediately bumps up the responsibility of the human doing the work—he gets to manage the bot.

It is not that the low-skilled jobs will disappear, and those people won't have any jobs left, but it is more about those people getting up-skilled in their own process. There are two reasons why this will be the case. First, companies are worrying about the competition that exists in their respective spaces. They don't want to give in to their competition just because they couldn't innovate. And that is why they are ready to reskill their workforce to keep up in the game. Second, technology is evolving every year and every quarter for them. Having a dearth of people with the right skills pushes them behind, which gives a chance to the unemployed to get the required skills and meet that demand. We have to provide 'data literacy' to the workforce for them to evolve in their work. Interpretation of data is what could become the nature of work in the next group of jobs.

---

167. James Manyika et al., "Help wanted: The future of work in advanced economies," McKinsey Global Institute, March 2012.

So, for low-skilled employees, instead of doing their job manually, companies adopt automation for the repetitive tasks and those employees get promoted to apply cognitive abilities at work. They have an opportunity to learn coding and the technology behind operating those robots. When I think about digital transformation in the sense of the three steps of digitization, digitalization, and digital transformation, it is about achieving digitalization at this point.

I interviewed a senior official from a retail company in India. He leads his North India's supply chain and procurement arm of the company. While discussing automations, we stumbled upon the utopian vision that he, as a leader, wishes to have for his team. His first wish was doing away with the functional training of his team. With RPA taking care of the procurement plans, most of the purchase orders that are, otherwise, manually filled in an excel sheet, can be generated by a software. So, instead of using manpower for filling forms, he wants the cognitive abilities of the supply chain folks to focus on negotiating costs with vendors and developing ways to shorten the lead time of procurement. He wants to promote people who are smart to anticipate changes with seasonal demands or shocks like the pandemic. That is the kind of cognitive ability that he wishes to develop in his team.

3. *Evolution of customer empathy*

Machines are getting smarter. They know their owner's usage patterns and many times they can anticipate their owner's needs, even when an ambiguous order is given to them. For example, your Google accounts are so well connected that when you tell your maps, "Take me home," you wouldn't expect it to ask you for more details before quickly prompting you a path. With smart home devices getting common, our grocery lists are merged with our Fitbit details and our food orders are mapped with the route we take to work. You might mind some of the data your phone is picking up, but that's AI for you.

If manufacturers think from a customer point of view, they will realize that the customer never wants to move out of their comfort zone. You can either add to that comfort zone or make something of your own that is so much more comfortable for them that they decide to shift to your digital environment. Of course, the latter is highly risky and requires more time and effort to build. In a factory, IoT is mostly used for maintenance and limited warehousing purposes. That's where you require a lot of devices to talk to each other and predict behaviors. This automation or predictive support is not merely the realm of high-end, big-ticket devices. Nor it is solely used to signal when something is wrong. It is also a function of ongoing assistance—to help with regular tasks that are now manual or lifestyle concerns like health and safety.

In a similar way, the customers also want things to be extremely simplified for them. The more thinking your device does, the less it is required for the customers to do. That's a big part of customer delight nowadays. You want a simple three step solution to your problem instead of a sixty-minute phone call. That is where the smart devices diagnose the problem by themselves and can predict the right solution.

Currently, there are twenty-six billion devices that make up the worldwide IoT. That number is expected to balloon to seventy-five billion by 2025.[168] Not all of those integrations would run smoothly. Some mechanical problems will still

---

168. "80 Insightful Internet of Things Statistics (Infographic)," Safeatlast, accessed October 6, 2020.

need a human touch. What would change is how you receive that support. With IoT devices sending and receiving massive amounts of data when you reach out, via chat or phone, the service will be far more personalized.[169]

Major industries where customer centric operations take place are hospitality, healthcare, FMCG, and electronics.[170] It may include an improvement in their product design processes or working on streamlining the logistics system. Product design is based on the digital twin created as a simulation of all the desirable factors that customers want in the product. Similarly, IoT sensor data combines the physical and digital logistics flow to share real-time trucking and inventory data between your logistics partners till the point of sale.

All of these solutions are meant to provide transparency of the process to the customer. If they can track their shipments from one place to another at a click of a button, they are relieved. If they know how much value they are receiving for a service in quantified terms, their trust in the service builds. Hence, the digital Lean is meant to create that simplified visual control for your customer—whether internal or external.

4. *Stronger KPIs, more sustainable transformation*

The successful companies would include process engineers who can help redesign fulfillment centers. They would depend on network optimization specialists who can optimize supply chains. As people in these profiles shape and manage your portfolio of digital products, they can ensure that each one is directly tied to the desired customer experience and your

169. Ibid.
170. Blake Morgan, "The 10 Most Customer-Obsessed Companies of 2019," *Forbes*, December 20, 2019.

planned business outcomes. Traditional success metrics would be recast across the organization: incentives, adoption, value, and performance will include the customer, and one set of metrics will cover multiple functions. Within a streamlined portfolio, different digital assets can even share product, price, promotion, and customer data from a single source, contributing to an edgeless experience at scale across platforms.[171]

Lean is more effective with cross-functions realizing same targets. When people from various positions in the end-to-end process chain come together to work on performance topics, they speak the same language and leverage the same way of working. Whether it is sales, marketing, product management, service, research & development, or manufacturing, they all know daily management and problem solving as well as the right leadership behavior and language around it. Ultimately, instead of working in islands, they are now able to build bridges. This is how Lean thinking becomes a crucial enabler in business transformation.[172]

One of the two Bill Gates rules of automation says "… [any] automation applied to an inefficient operation will [only] magnify the inefficiency."[173] Although Lean will survive the Industry 4.0 revolution and co-exist with the technology that underpins it, the shape and utilization of its technical solutions will not change. For instance, advancements in technology have transformed the traditional physical *Kanban* cards into e-Kanban and the paper-based value stream mapping into e-VSM. In other cases, Industry 4.0

171. Scott Buchchols, Bill Briggs, *Tech Trends—2020*, Deloitte Insights, January 15, 2020.

172. Ibid.

173. Christopher Stancombe, "Tempted to rewrite Bill Gates' rules on automation?," Capgemini, January 2, 2015.

technologies may require some Lean solutions to adapt to co-exist with such technologies, whereas the use of others may be reduced or disappear. For example, it is easy to envisage that highly digitalized and automated production environments will limit the use of whiteboards, physical *Kanban* cards, and *Andon* cords, among other Lean solutions.[174]

5. *Enhanced active feedback loop*

There is a simple process-concept that I learnt at Tata. And this concept was so widely used in my work that now I problem solve according to this principle. It is called the PDCA cycle, or plan-do-check-act. As the full form suggests, it includes a sequence of planning the project or the process steps first, which takes majority of the time. Then comes the execution of the plan. "Check" involves analyzing the metrics and discussing effectiveness of the applied changes with the team. The last step of "act" completes the feedback loop for the implementation. It involves going back and improving on the process to get better results.[175]

From a manufacturing standpoint, if product development is thought of as "plan" in a PDCA cycle, it becomes apparent how critical it is to apply Lean thinking during this lifecycle phase. The design phase should plan not only for the product, but also the value stream. This means understanding the product, process flow, material flow, and information flow, and integrating all of this understanding into a harmonious system.

---

174. Stephen Laaper, Brian Kiefer, "Digital lean manufacturing: Industry 4.0 technologies transform lean processes to advance the enterprise," Deloitte Insights, August 21, 2020.
175. "What is the Plan-Do-Check-Act (PDCA) Cylcle?," ASQ, accessed February 27, 2021.

In most of my what-if scenarios for Lean, I have concluded that the first thing to consider is the industry. It is what defines the mode of feedback and how will it undergo most transformation. There is a different level of digital maturity that different industries possess. Hence, the level of digitally enhanced feedback mechanism would be different too. Also, it wouldn't be fair to a mechanical industry to compare their progress with a software sector company.

6. *Data galore—sharing is caring*

We have already seen the power and importance of data in the chapters before. It is one of my top 7 picks which will change the course of Lean as we know it. As we move toward the oil wells of data for our analysis, the work gets tougher to do it manually. Data serves as a decision indicator to the analysts and internal strategy teams. If managed well, companies can put their investments to good use by anticipating the future. With the advent of IoT and Industry 4.0, the reality is that data is being generated at a staggering speed and at high volumes, creating a need for an infrastructure that can store and manage this data more efficiently.

This is where cloud computing comes in. Cloud computing offers a platform for users to store and process vast amounts of data on remote servers. It enables organizations to use computer resources without having to develop a computing infrastructure on premise. Manufacturers' global spending on cloud computing platforms is predicted to reach $9.2 billion in 2021, according to IDC.[176] A key factor

---

176. Kevyan Karimi et al., "Industry 4.0: 7 Real-World Examples of Digital Manufacturing in Action," Autonomous Manufacturing, March 28, 2019.

behind this adoption is the benefit of being able to centralize operations, eliminating unwanted reworks and delays so
that information can be shared across an entire organization.
Nutanix predicted in 2019 that the adoption rate of cloud
computing in manufacturing firms would more than double
from 19 percent to 45 percent in 2021.[177] This means that traditional IT infrastructure, which manufacturing controlled
within their factories, is poised to blow out on a global scale
through cloud. I'm talking about data on a computer hard
drive blowing open to cloud-stored data that can be accessed
globally at the same time.

Different companies operate through public and private
cloud sharing. In the case of a private cloud, which is also
known as an internal or enterprise cloud, it resides on a company's intranet or hosted data center where all the company's data is protected behind a firewall. Unfortunately, the
main drawback with a private cloud is that all management,
maintenance, and updating of data centers is the owner's
responsibility.[178]

With a public cloud, the management of a public cloud
hosting solution is not the company's responsibility. It is
managed by a third-party provider who is responsible for
the maintenance of the data center. However, security is an
element that companies can feel to be lacking in a public
cloud. At the end of the day, it all boils down to control.
This is where hybrid cloud solutions come into play. Hybrid
cloud solutions can provide a path by providing backup storage on off-premises for conservation, protecting data from

177. Joanie Wexler, "Elusive Hybrid Cloud Tops IT Wish Lists," Nutanix,
November 30, 2020.

178. Anil Prabha, "Are hybrid cloud solutions a win for SMEs?," *TechHQ*,
March 4, 2019.

corruption, and establishing documentation that outlines the reliable data recovery process. Basically, they are currently the best choice since they give you the best of both worlds.

Cloud enables Lean in many applications. Take connected cars for example. Volkswagen was among the first companies to jump into this technology for their products and has partnered with Microsoft to work with similar "automotive cloud" for itself.[179] It aims to add over five million Volkswagen brand offerings per year to its IoT with the help of this cloud service by 2022.[180] It helps a faster and more controlled operations since data has a strong base for making these cars.

Sharing data has its merits for a physical environment like manufacturing, which is changing every day. With data sharing, we can see the silos being broken down. Customer service responses may feed into design choices. Production schedules may be adjusted on-the-fly to reflect supply chain realities. Entirely new business models may emerge from the synchronous integration of departments that had previously worked in series or parallel.

7. *Get on the floor and Lean on*

At Tata, we used to do *Gemba* walks to determine the health of our processes. A *Gemba* walk is an essential part of the Lean management philosophy. *Gemba* stands for "actual place" in Japanese, which simply means taking cognizance of the actual location where improvement or *Kaizen* is being performed. Its initial purpose is to allow managers and leaders to observe the actual work process, engage with

---

179. Edward Taylor, "VW deepens cloud computing partnership with Microsoft," Automotive News, February 27, 2019.
180. Ibid.

employees, gain knowledge about the work process, and explore opportunities for continuous improvement.

In the end, to create a change, you have to roll up your sleeves and experience the ground realities. Whether you are a practitioner or owner of a project, *Gemba* still applies. Being present as an analyst is a primary duty of the Lean practitioner, which will never change even in the future for most of the industries. It is like any standup meeting (or "morning meeting" in some cases), which the teams do to start the day with a to-do list and end the day with a recap. Getting on the shop floor is the most effective way to observe a process and plan for continuous improvement. *Gemba* basically involves three essential steps: "Go and see, ask why, and respect people."[181] My mentor from Tata was a religious follower of this exercise. Even after he became a manufacturing head and had a team of two hundred managers at his disposal to pick a team and do a *Gemba* for him, he continued doing it himself. I can estimate that a minimum of ten problems would get resolved through his daily *Gemba*, which would have otherwise come at his desk a week later.

To sum this up in a single sentence: To understand, you need to see, identify the problems, and create action plans to solve them.[182]

These seven trends are not the only ones that would influence the future of Lean but cover the major changes in the value chain—input, processes, and output with a base on elements of information and skill.

---

181. "Gemba Walk: Where the Real Work Happens," Kanbanize, accessed February 27, 2021.

182. "What is Gemba and what is its importance in Lean Manufacturing?," Think Lean Six Sigma, accessed February 27, 2021.

CHAPTER 14

CONCLUSION

———

Skills direct behavior for a known situation.

When you get into an unknown and uncertain situation, skills don't always apply, so we lean on our attributes. Business and skill development are both infinite games. There is no start or finish and there are definitely no winners. To overcome uncertainty, there are different mindsets used by a finite and an infinite player. The finite player likes to train and prepare, so that he eliminates unknowns. Finite minded players fear the unknown and uncertainty, so they practice, practice, and practice. Think of athletes and people in the military who are prepared for any eventuality. Unfortunately, the problem is that it only works for expected things. An unforeseen situation throws the finite player into a tizzy while the infinite minded player embraces uncertainty. It is no more muscle memory.[183] "I didn't have to think, I just relied on my

---

183. Simon Sinek, "The Infinite Game: How to Lead in the 21st Century," May 13, 2019, video, 1:31:19.

training," you hear it all the time, where the infinite-minded thinker, at the time of uncertainty, begins thinking.

Lean has a similar situation for Lean practitioners at many stages. Evolution is a necessary evil. I call it evil as Lean is a flag-bearer of small but continuous improvements, which can lead to chaos if the change is not handled with care. However, cases in tech advancement are, more often than not, revolutionary. They pose to create a new trend for the next three to five years, and then disappear. In my exploration of Lean's future, I encountered this dilemma multiple times—whether I should call the next phase of Lean "digital Lean" or "hybrid Lean."

From what I explored, I found a lot of disparity between the mindset of people thinking about Lean from a perspective of services and product making. Although many of the challenges are known by the teams already, it is still hard to remove all of them completely due to varying factors from the external market and competitive pressures to a slow-moving internal administration. It is really hard to erase everything and just hit refresh. To overcome the barriers, it is the intention to continually improve, that matters the most.

Lean, if upgraded and armed with data in the right direction, can reduce the effort to understand operations and generate more accurate, precise, and timely information. It is more than a set of Industry 4.0 tools—it encompasses reevaluating current processes, using a digital mindset, changing behaviors, and shifting decision-making. It transforms from experience-based to a mix of experience and data-based, far more efficiently than Lean processes alone could ever do. So how should one start with this right now?

Thinking big is a plausible step for the decision makers. Sometimes, if we go too much into a jargon, we miss the whole point of the philosophy. What does Lean entail in the long run? Is it designed to create step improvements in your bottom line, increase cash flow, or just cover a part of the company? Do you need to think that your company is at the digitization stage or close to digital transformation? Is there an operational requirement or did you just come out of a bedazzling meeting and think of Lean as a good way to start something aspirational? You need to answer these questions, or rather choose the question that relates to you and start a change.

Once you are done with that decision, you need to start small. Start somewhere where the solution can capture measurable value-addition and where the people, process, and technology are ready for change. We already do it in the implementation phase, and at least that would remain a constant in future. An already extremely high-performing production line may enjoy benefits from digital Lean, but such benefits will likely be less than ideal for an initial pilot that is bearing the cost of development of capabilities. Good places to start often include complete production lines or assets (a process, value stream, or sub-value stream) with a clear bottleneck. Although this book had a focus on creating an awareness of possible changes in Lean methodology with tech advancements, I really enjoyed reviewing E. M. Goldratt's *The Goal*, which talks about the theory of constraints.[184] Theory of constraints still applies well as a Lean tool and acts as a first step if you are trying to jump on a moving project and want to get hold of the bottleneck quickly.

---

184. Eliyahu M. Goldratt, *The Goal: A Process of Ongoing Improvement—25th Anniversary Edition* (Great Barrington—The North River Press, 2012), 271-312.

Another area is the people and organizations that create awareness and trainings. In my variety-filled experience, internal trainings proved to be much more efficient and cost-effective than those done through external resources. This ensures two things: first, the organization gains people who believe in change and can prepare them quickly within teams, and second, it helps in creating an inventory of knowledge for the future. Believe in your team leader if they ask you to attend trainings. Every refresher course that you participate in will reset your vision for analyzing your process. You can get a eureka moment just by talking to more people and learning about their perspective. Man is a social animal and should use that quality well! Right?

The final achievement milestone is scaling fast. Not all scaled Lean efforts generate enough value to meet the business case. An initial pilot is important to define the right direction for rest of the development. A feedback mechanism is important to increase customer-driven precision. Each scaled pilot helps realize value and build the capabilities that are defined while thinking big. Determine the order of assets, lines, or plants to scale, then develop and execute plans accordingly during the pilot. But, keep recording the best practices and move onto the next area.

In conclusion, to reiterate with what I started above, we are all in a situation that throws us into the infinite and uncertain future. The companies led by leaders with an "infinite mind" will embrace this uncertainty. Elon Musk started a decade ago with Tesla cars and now has the most valuable company on Earth.[185] He is just one example of

185. Sergie Klebnikov, "Tesla is Now the World's Most Valuable Car Company with a $208 Billion Valuation," *Forbes,* July 1, 2020.

that infinite mindset. I hope we can find more of such successes from my readers and that this knowledge is helpful and inspiring for you to take that first step in revolutionary thinking. Go out and win the world.

ACKNOWLEDGEMENTS

This book was a result of passion, grit, and relentlessness. None of this could come without the constant support I had from everyone throughout my twelve month writing journey.

I started with an inquisitive mind to apply what I had learnt over the years, but now I'm fortunate to help every reader with my study on Lean. This book would not have been possible without the guidance, help, and constant support over the years by Mr. Anal Vijay Singh and Prof. Eric Koester. The former was my *Sensei* at Tata Motors, from whom I learnt the most, and the latter, an inspirational mentor who discovered this creative side of me.

I want to thank my professors and seniors who guided me with their innovative case studies and insights in their classes that helped me get attracted to operations. Thanks to my cousin, Mohit Mittal, dearest friends, Kavish Munim, Bimal Prakash, and Shruti Rawat, my senior Bhavik Mistry, and my former colleague Pankaj Bhandari, who were constantly helpful in providing me ideas not only for the book but also about how to pave my way as a first time author.

I'm grateful to Derek Leong who connected me with such

insightful professionals that I could not fathom to have met on my own.

It takes a village to write a book. My village was the team at the Creator Institute and New Degree Press, especially Eric Koester and Brian Bies. I found special friends in fellow authors, Felix Dey, Charlene, Galo Bowen, and Daisy Bugarin with whom I could compare my progress. Also, a special shout-out to my editors Katie Sigler and Paige Buxbaum for keeping me on track for over a year.

This book would not have been a reality if I didn't have the support of the numerous beta-readers and contributors of this project, including:

Abhigyan Smit
Abhinav Pachauri
Abhishek Pandey
Abra Sitler
Aditya Kumar Sharma
Akash Kang
Akshay Grewal
Amirali Sewani
Amitabh Rai
Anant Shrivastava
Anil Kumar Gupta
Ankita Sur
Anthony Ingelido
Ashwin Dakshinamurthi
Audrey del Rosario
Bhargav Shankar
Bhavik Mistry
Bimal Prakash
Bryan Crosson

Callie Wilkinson
Canan Ulu
Daniel Ingram
Daniela Matielo
Darshana Sarmah
Derek Leong
Dhruv Vikrant Singh
Dipanshu Jain
Ekta Vohra
Elizabeth Powell
Eric Koester
Erika Wohl
Estevan Astorga
Felix Dey
Gabe Nelson
Galo Bowen
Gautam Jain
Gopika Spaenle
Gordon Bradshaw

Gurmeet Anil
Harshit Mehta
Homero Soto
Jared Koch
Jayati Takkar
Jayson Varkey
Joshua Crouse
Junior Mwemba
Kasra Ferdows
Kaushik Kashyap
Kavish Munim
Keisuke Adachi
Kevin Schlosser
Khushboo Poddar
Komal Shah
Koundilya Desiraju
Kuushagra Mittal
Kyle Angelos
Loretta Richardson
Mahesh Kundu
Manas Chitransh
Mansi Tewari
Michael Wathen
Michelle Wu
Mohit Mittal
Nandika Monga
Neha Mundra
Nicholas Reasner
Pankaj Bhandari
Patricia Rivera
Pavan Agarwal
Piyush Arora

Prachi Jindal
Prajwal Kapinadka
Prashant Malaviya
Purva Monga
Ravi Nagpal
Ritika Gupta
Rohan Dalvi
Rohit Kumar
Romen Chowdhury
Saawan Bangur
Sadheerth Vijayakumar
Sagar Rastogi
Sanchi Wadhwa
Satya Agarwal
Shreya Sahay
Sid Kashyap
Smriti Gupta
Soumik Manik
Stefanie Cohen
Stella Sitt
Sudarshan Soma
Summi Sinha
Swapna Singhal
Tauseef Bari
Thomas Gage
Tsai-Hsuan Teng
Vaibhav Palav
Vaibhav Tripathi
Vaibhav Varma
Viplav Kirti
Vivek Verma

People

Anal Singh   Gary Weber
Ankur Gupta   Kevin Schlosser
Ashrae Sahni   Pradeesh Wanniarachchi
Barnali Sarkar   Rishav Banerjee
Bob Rush   Savita Gupta
Derek Leong   Tony Ingelido

Lastly, lots of love to my parents and my sister for their moral support and blessings.

Mohit Gupta

APPENDIX

Chapter (ii)—Introduction

Agile Alliance. "What is Agile?" Accessed September 8, 2020. https://www.agilealliance.org/agile101/.

Desoutter Tools. "Industrial Revolution—From Industry 1.0 to Industry 4.0." Accessed September 8, 2020. https://www.desouttertools.com/industry-4-0/news/503/industrial-revolution-from-industry-1-0-to-industry-4-0.

Enterprise IoT Insights. "State of Things | Smart Manufacturing (Part 3): Use Case Modelling." Accessed September 8,2020. https://enterpriseiotinsights.com/20190214/channels/news/state-of-things-smart-manufacturing-part-3-use-case-modelling.

Kitchen Nightmares. "Fine Dining is a Fine Mess | Kitchen Nightmares." January 27, 2021. Video. 4:10. https://www.youtube.com/watch?v=MA9yBOogQ3w.

Morgan, Blake. "100 Stats on Digital Transformation and Customer Experience." *Forbes.* December 16, 2019. https://www.forbes.com/sites/blakemorgan/2019/12/16/100-stats-on-digital-transformation-and-customer-experience/?sh=299273a63bf3.

Roof, Katie. "Elon Musk Says, 'Humans are Underrated,' Calls Tesla's 'Excessive Automation' a 'Mistake'." TechCrunch. April 13, 2018. https://techcrunch.com/2018/04/13/elon-musk-says-humans-are-underrated-calls-teslas-excessive-automation-a-mistake/.

Soper, Taylor and Nat Levy. "Amazon to Acquire Ring Video Doorbell Maker, Cracking Open the Door in Home Security Market." *GeekWire*. February 27, 2018. https://www.geekwire.com/2018/amazon-acquire-ring-video-doorbell-maker-cracking-open-door-home-security-market/.

Chapter 1—Lean: Past and Present

Agile Manifesto. "History: The Agile Manifesto." Accessed August 10, 2020. https://agilemanifesto.org/history.html.

Gilberth, Frank B., and Ernestine Gilberth Carey. *Cheaper by the Dozen*. New York: Thomas Y. Crowell Co., 1948.

Goodreads. "Cheaper by the Dozen Quotes." Accessed January 10, 2021, https://www.goodreads.com/work/quotes/1925199-cheaper-by-the-dozen.

Graban, Mark. "A Lean Slaughterhouse?" *Lean Blog* (blog). Last Updated Dec 12, 2012. https://www.leanblog.org/2008/09/lean-slaughterhouse/.

Harris, Laquita. "Lean Manufacturing Made Toyota the Success Story it is Today." RCBI. April 2008. http://www.rcbi.org/index.php/viewarticle/130-capacity-magazine/spring-2007/features/336-lean-manufacturing-made-toyota-the-success-story-it-is-todayinvesting-in-our-economy.

Joy, Manu. "Lean Leadership." *Researchgate* (blog). April 2019. https://www.researchgate.net/publication/332275920_Lean_Leadership.

Lean Enterprise Institute (blog). "A Brief History of Lean." Accessed August 10, 2020. https://www.lean.org/whatslean/history.cfm.

Leanscape (blog). "The 8 Wastes of Lean—Stop Wasting Your Resources." August 20, 2020. Accessed August 25, 2020. https://www.leanscape.io/8-wastes-of-lean/.

Leonardo Group Americas, "How Piggly Wiggly Revolutionized Manufacturing, or the Quite Genius of a Milk Rack," Medium, Feb 04, 2015. https://medium.com/@LeonardoGroupAmericas/how-piggly-wiggly-revolutionized-manufacturing-6ae7e76af184.

Lumen Learning. "Reading: Taylor and the Gilberths." Accessed August 10, 2020. https://courses.lumenlearning.com/wmintrobusiness/chapter/reading-fredrick-taylors-scientific-management-2/.

PBS. "Ford installs First Moving Assembly Line 1913." Accessed August 10, 2020. https://www.pbs.org/wgbh/aso/databank/entries/dt13as.html.

Science. "Assembly Line." Accessed August 10, 2020. https://science.jrank.org/pages/558/Assembly-Line-History.html.

Skhmot, Nawras. "The 8 Wastes of Lean." The Lean Way. August 5, 2017. https://theleanway.net/The-8-Wastes-of-Lean.

Wilson, Mike. "Going Lean: IKEA style." Creative Safety Supply (blog). February 21, 2013. https://blog.creativesafetysupply.com/going-lean-ikea-style/.

Chapter 2—Hors d'oeuvre—Stories on Lean Jargon

Agile Alliance. "Kanban." Accessed September 9, 2020. https://www.agilealliance.org/glossary/kanban/.

American Society for Quality. "What are the Five Ss (5S) of Lean." Accessed September 9, 2020. https://asq.org/quality-resources/lean/five-s-tutorial.

Do, Doanh. "What is Muda, Mura, and Muri?" The Lean Way. August 5, 2017. https://theleanway.net/muda-mura-muri.

Roser, Christopher. "What Exactly is Jidoka?" All About Lean. July 17, 2018. https://www.allaboutlean.com/jidoka-1.

Skhmot, Nawras. "The 8 Wastes of Lean." The Lean Way. August 5, 2017. https://theleanway.net/The-8-Wastes-of-Lean.

The Trailer Guy. "The Karate Kid (1984)—Movie Trailer." October 10, 2010. Video. 2:11. https://www.youtube.com/watch?v=P9fdU78SpA8.

White, Sarah K. "What is Kaizen? A Business Strategy Focused on Improvement." *CIO.* July 16, 2019. https://www.cio.com/article/3408780/what-is-kaizen-a-business-strategy-focused-on-improvement.html.

Chapter 3—Software is Eating the World

Canales, Katie. "Ousted Uber Cofounder Travis Kalanick has Reportedly Spent $130 Million on his Ghost Kitchen Startup. Here's What It's Like Inside One of the Secretive Locations." *Businessinsider.* October 20, 2020. https://www.businessinsider.com/cloud-kitchens-travis-kalanick-san-francisco-location-address-pictures-2019-11.

Chatzky, Jean. "A Non-Boring History of Coupons." Retailmenot. September 1, 2015. https://www.retailmenot.com/blog/sc-history-of-coupons.html.

Coggle. "Dominos Operations." Infographic. Accessed October 29, 2020. https://coggle.it/diagram/W4dpWYdcxrRvRpDo/t/operations-at-dominos.

Dillon, Sunny, and Kevin Wu. "Delivery 2.0: How on-demand meal services will become something far bigger." Fast Company. February 15, 2021. https://www.fastcompany.com/90604082/

future-of-on-demand-meal-delivery-ghost-kitchens-postmates-
doordash-uber-eats.

Keesling, Adam. "How Domino's Won the Pandemic." Marker (blog).
May 24, 2020. https://marker.medium.com/how-dominos-
won-the-pandemic-e5f0929cb5dd.

Montgomery, April, and Ken Mingis. "The Evolution of Apple's
iPhone." *Computerworld*. October 15, 2020.
https://www.computerworld.com/article/2604020/the-evolu-
tion-of-apples-iphone.html.

Munroe, Tony. "Alibaba.com Shares Soar in Trading Debut."
Reuters. November 5, 2007. https://www.reuters.com/article/
tech-alibabacom-ipo-dc/alibaba-com-shares-soar-in-trading-
debut-idUKHKG31215920071106.

Netflix. "The Social Dilemma." January 26,2020. Video. 1:34:36.
https://www.netflix.com/title/81254224.

Qualtrics. "What is Voice of the Customer (VoC)?" Accessed
October 29, 2020. https://www.qualtrics.com/experience-
management/customer/what-is-voice-of-customer/.

Roomer, Jari. "3 Reasons Why You Shouldn't Check Your Phone
Within 1 Hour of Waking Up." Medium (Blog). July 31, 2019.
https://medium.com/personal-growth-lab/3-reasons-why-you-
shouldnt-check-your-smartphone-within-1-hour-of-waking-
up-6ccb1264ec74.

Segan, Sascha. "A Visual History of the Motorola Razr." *PCMag*.
November 13, 2019. https://www.pcmag.com/news/a-visual-
history-of-the-motorola-razr.

Selecthub. "Manufacturing Process Software: How It Works."
Accessed October 29, 2020. https://www.selecthub.com/enter-
prise-resource-planning/manufacturing-process-software/.

Sharda, Naveen. "Serving Food from the Cloud." Toptal.
Accessed October 29, 2020. https://www.toptal.com/finance/
growth-strategy/cloud-kitchen.

Weliver, David. "Meal Delivery Comparison: Home Chef vs. HelloFresh vs. Blue Apron vs. Freshly vs. EveryPlate vs. Sunbasket." Money Under 30. Last modified: February 7, 2021. https://www.moneyunder30.com/meal-delivery-comparison.

Chapter 4—Case Study: Auto Industry Exploration— Where it All Started

Awasare, Anant. "How to Calculate Standard Time by Using MOST Maynard Operation Sequence Technique." May 31, 2018. Video. 6:24. https://www.youtube.com/watch?v=TPkhxWAJvPw.

Blue Robotics. "Our Story." Accessed August 5, 2020. https://bluerobotics.com/about.

Faraday Future. "Experience a New Species—Faraday Future." Accessed August 1, 2020. https://www.ff.com/.

Flashback FM. "Neo—'The One' | The Matrix [Open Matte]." November 11, 2016. Video. 3:58. https://www.youtube.com/watch?v=H-0RHqDWcJE.

Henshell, Adam. "Improve Organization with 5S: The Theory Behind Marie Kondo." Process.st. March 15, 2019. https://www.process.st/5s/.

Immerman, Graham. "Elon Musk Focusing on Tesla Lean Manufacturing." Machine Metrics. February 20, 2018. https://www.machinemetrics.com/blog/elon-musk-focusing-on-tesla-lean-manufacturing.

Lean Factories. "The Lean Transformation of Tesla and Elon Musk." Accessed August 5, 2020. https://leanfactories.com/the-lean-transformation-of-tesla-and-elon-musk.

O'Kane, Sean. "Hyundai Will Build Electric Vehicles With EV Startup Canoo." *The Verge*. February 11, 2020.

https://www.theverge.com/2020/2/11/21133461/hyundai-canoo-electric-cars-partership-kia.

Yamaha Motors India. "Products—Yamaha." Accessed August 1, 2020. https://www.yamaha-motor-india.com/two-wheeler.html.

Chapter 5—Digital vs Physical

Buchholz, Scott, and Bill Briggs. "Tech Trends—2020." Deloitte Insights. January 15, 2020. https://www2.deloitte.com/content/dam/Deloitte/cz/Documents/technology/DI_TechTrends2020.pdf.

Caudron, Jo, and Dado Van Peteghem. *Digital Transformation: A Model to Master Digital Disruption* (Belgium: Duval Union Consulting, January 2014.

Dahl, Jacob, Ervin Ng, and Joydeep Sengupta. "How Asia is Reinventing Banking for the Digital Age." McKinsey. February 11, 2020. https://www.mckinsey.com/featured-insights/asia-pacific/how-asia-is-reinventing-banking-for-the-digital-age.

Dwoskin, Elizabeth. "Americans Might Never Come Back to the Office, and Twitter is Leading the Charge." *The Washington Post.* October 1, 2020. https://www.washingtonpost.com/technology/2020/10/01/twitter-work-from-home/?arc404=true.

Edwards, David. "Amazon Now Has 200,000 Robots Working in its Warehouses." *Robotics & Automation News.* January 21, 2020. https://roboticsandautomationnews.com/2020/01/21/amazon-now-has-200000-robots-working-in-its-warehouses/28840.

Finextra. "Most Banks Will Be Made Irrelevant by 2030—Gartner." October 29, 2018. https://www.finextra.com/newsarticle/32860/most-banks-will-be-made-irrelevant-by-2030---gartner.

Iqbal, Mansoor. "App Download and Usage Statistics (2020)." Business of Apps. October 30, 2020. https://www.businessofapps.com.

International Data Corporation. "Worldwide Spending on Cognitive and Artificial Intelligence Systems Forecast to Reach $77.6 Billion in 2022, According to New IDC Spending Guide." September 19, 2018.

Prater, Meg. "25 Google Search Statistics to Bookmark ASAP." Hubspot (blog). Accessed Sep 12, 2020. https://blog.hubspot.com/marketing/google-search-statistics.

Rudden, Jennifer. "Number of Unicorns Worldwide as of January 2020, by Country." Statista. Feb 7, 2020. https://www.statista.com/statistics/1096928/number-of-global-unicorns-by-country.

Schoolov, Katie. "How Amazon Gets Prime Day Orders to Your House in Just One Day." *CNBC*. July 13, 2019. https://www.cnbc.com/2019/07/12/how-amazon-gets-prime-day-orders-to-your-house-in-just-one-day.html.

Wattles, Jackie. "Amazon Starts One-day Shipping for Millions of Products." *CNN Business*. June 3, 2019. https://www.cnn.com/2019/06/03/business/amazon-one-day-shipping.

Chapter 6—The Beyond | Lean for Service Industry

Babu, Bharat. "Competitive Position Analysis of Airtel." *Medium* (Blog). November 7, 2020. https://bharathbabu68.medium.com/competitive-position-analysis-of-airtel-e6424be24478#

Feather. "About Feather." Accessed November 10, 2020. https://www.livefeather.com/about.

Hagel III, John, John Seely Brown, and Lang Davison. "Why Do Companies Exist?" *Harvard Business Review*. February 25, 2009. https://hbr.org/2009/02/why-do-companies-exist.html.

Hanna, Julia. "Bringing 'Lean' Principles to Service Industries." Harvard Business School. October 22, 2007. https://hbswk.hbs.edu/item/bringing-lean-principles-to-service-industries.

Khanna, Tarun. "China + India: The Power of Two." *Harvard Business Review*. December 2007. https://hbr.org/2007/12/china-india-the-power-of-two.

Success Mortgage Partners Inc. "Loan Process." Accessed November 11, 2020. https://www.successmortgagepartners.com/loan-process/#.

Wanniarachchi, Pradeesh. "Can We Apply Lean Six Sigma in Service Industry?" Linkedin. June 14, 2020. https://www.linkedin.com/pulse/can-we-apply-lean-six-sigma-service-industry-pradeesh-wanniarachchi-/.

Chapter 7—Lean Projects: Challenges and Myths

Bastin, Zach, Albert Sang, and Ashrae Sahni. "There is No Quick Pay-off from Lean." AlixPartners. September 15, 2020. https://www.alixpartners.com/insights-impact/insights/theres-no-quick-payoff-from-lean/.

Canoo. "Canoo: Electric Lifestyle, Sport and Working Vehicles." Accessed October 6, 2020. https://www.canoo.com/.

Cornelissen, Ruben. "What are the Main Challenges When Implementing Lean and How Do Industry and Company Characteristics Influence These Challenges?" Wageningen University. November 23, 2013. https://edepot.wur.nl/286448.

Faraday Future. "Faraday Future: Experience a New Species." Accessed October 6, 2020. https://www.ff.com/.

McKinsey Global Institute. "The Internet of Things: Mapping the Value Beyond the Hype." June 2015. https://www.mckinsey.com/~/media/McKinsey/Industries/Technology.

Overby, Stephanie, Lynn Greiner, and Lauren Gibbons Paul. "What is an SLA? Best Practices for Service-level Agreements." *CIO*.

July 5, 2017. https://www.cio.com/article/2438284/outsourcing-sla-definitons-and-solutions.html.

Chapter 8—Case Study: Ground Realities—Boeing's Lean Implementation

Boeing. "Historical Snapshot." Accessed October 29, 2020. https://www.boeing.com/history/products/737-classic.page.

Brady, Chris. "Production." The Boeing 737 Technical Site. September 1999. http://www.b737.org.uk/index.htm.

Tully, Shawn. "Boeing Must Transform the Way It Builds Planes." *Fortune.* March 8, 1993. https://fortune.com/1993/03/08/boeing-planes-manufacturing/.

Chapter 9—The New Oil | In Data We Trust?

Beg, Aamer, Bryce Hall, Paul Jenkins, Eric Lamarre and Brian McCarthy. "The COVID-19 Recovery Will Be Digital: A Plan for the First 90 Days." McKinsey Digital. May 14, 2020. https://www.mckinsey.com/business-functions/mckinsey-digital/our-insights/the-covid-19-recovery-will-be-digital-a-plan-for-the-first-90-days.

Birch, Scott. "Deloitte: Scaling Digital Technologies in Manufacturing." Manufacturing Global. October 2, 2020. https://www.manufacturingglobal.com/digital-factory/deloitte-scaling-digital-technologies-manufacturing.

Bova, Tiffany. "Customer Focus with Tifanny Bova." Webinar, AT&T Externship 2020, Online, July 15, 2020. https://about.att.com/inside_connections_blog/2020/att_summer_learning_academy.html.

Dhawan, Rajat, Kunvar Singh, and Ashish Tuteja. "When Big Data Goes Lean." McKinsey & Company. February 1, 2014. https://www.mckinsey.com/business-functions/operations/our-insights/when-big-data-goes-lean.

Heilweil, Rebecca. "Tinder May Not Get You a Date. It Will Get Your Data." *Vox*. February 14, 2020. https://www.vox.com/recode/2020/2/14/21137096/how-tinder-matches-work-algorithm-grindr-bumble-hinge-algorithms.

IBM Education. "Monte Carlo Simulation." Accessed February 27, 2021. https://www.ibm.com/cloud/learn/monte-carlo-simulation.

Kanbanize. "5 Whys: The Ultimate Root Cause Analysis Tool." Accessed February 20, 2021. https://kanbanize.com/lean-management/improvement/5-whys-analysis-tool.

Kruse, Kevin. "The 80/20 Rule and How It Can Change Your Life." *Forbes*. March 7, 2016. https://www.forbes.com/sites/kevinkruse/2016/03/07/80-20-rule/?sh=523a012b3814.

Logi Analytics. "What is Embedded Analytics?" Accessed February 28, 2021. https://www.logianalytics.com/definitiveguidetoembedded/what-is-embedded-analytics.

Murray, Adam. "How Can Manufacturing Data Help Your Organization?" Sisense. January 13, 2020. https://www.sisense.com/blog/how-can-manufacturing-data-help-your-organization.

Srinivasan, Prema. "How to Use Big Data Analytics to Supercharge Lean Manufacturing." PTC. September 3, 2020. https://www.ptc.com/en/blogs/iiot/how-to-use-big-data-analytics-to-supercharge-lean-manufacturing.

Chapter 10—The Potential of AI and ML

Agence France-Presse, "GE Says, 'Industrial Internet' Could be Worth Trillions," Industry Week, November 26, 2012. https://www.industryweek.com/technology-and-iiot/systems-integration/article/21958940/ge-says-industrial-internet-could-be-worth-trillions.

Altexsoft (blog). "Demand Forecasting Methods: Using Machine Learning and Predictive Analytics to See the Future of Sales." November 11, 2019. Accessed December 20, 2020. https://www.altexsoft.com/blog/demand-forecasting-methods-using-machine-learning/.

Bousetta, Alex. "Does Lean Six Sigma Need AI and ML?" LinkedIn. August 21, 2018. https://www.linkedin.com/pulse/when-does-process-improvement-lean-six-sigma-need-ai-alex-boussetta/.

Cruise Automation. "The Integrated Engineering Challenge of our Generation." Accessed October 31, 2020. https://www.getcruise.com/technology.

Garza-Reyes, Jose Arturo. "The Future of Manufacturing—Industry 4.0." The Future Factory. Accessed February 21, 2021. https://www.thefuturefactory.com/blog/47.

Irpan, Alex. "AlphaGo vs Lee Sedol: Post Match Commentaries." Sorta Insightful (blog). March 17, 2016. https://www.alexirpan.com/2016/03/17/alphago-lsd.html.

Koch, Christof. "How the Computer Beat the Go Master." Scientific American. March 19, 2016. https://www.scientificamerican.com/article/how-the-computer-beat-the-go-master/.

Laaper, Stephen, Brian Keifer. "Digital Lean Manufacturing—Industry 4.0 Technologies Transform Lean Processes to Advance the Enterprise." Deloitte Insights. August 21, 2020. https://www2.deloitte.com/us/en/insights/focus/industry-4-0/digital-lean-manufacturing.html.

Quibell, Andrew. "Lean Management Meets Artificial Intelligence, Machine Learning, the Internet of All Things." Lean Enterprise Institute. April 16, 2018. https://www.lean.org/LeanPost/Posting.cfm?LeanPostId=856.

Rao, Anand, Flavio Palaci, and Wilson Chao. "This is what the world's CEOs really think of AI." World Economic Forum. June 25, 2019. https://www.weforum.org/agenda/2019/06/ai-will-shape-our-future-how-do-we-ensure-it-is-used-responsibly/.

Rumsen, Ruby. "The Johari Window." *E-Learning Network* (blog). February 15, 2018. https://www.eln.io/blog/the-johari-window.

Walker, Nell. "Why a Bill of Materials is important." Manufacturing Global (blog). December 14, 2020. https://www.manufacturingglobal.com/lean-manufacturing/why-bill-materials-important.

Chapter 11—Confluence of the Future of Manufacturing | Lean and Agile

Bizagi. "How CIOs can Enable an Agile Organization." September 12, 2018. https://www.bizagi.com/en/blog/agile-and-low-code/how-cios-can-enable-an-agile-organization.

Boiser, Lena. "What is Lean Agile Project Management?" Kanban Zone. April 21, 2020. https://kanbanzone.com/2020/what-is-lean-agile-project-management/.

Canitz, Henry. "Lean Principles and Sales & Operations Planning (S&OP)," Logility. Accessed February 21, 2020. https://www.logility.com/blog/lean-principles-and-sales-operations-planning-sop/.

Delos Santos, and Jose Maria. "Agile vs. Waterfall: Differences in Software Development Methodologies?" Project Management. August 20, 2020.

Heller, Martha. "How Comcast IT moved from order-taker to innovator." *CIO.* December 2, 2020. https://www.cio.com/article/3598075/how-comcast-it-moved-from-order-taker-to-innovator.html.

High, Peter. "Comcast CIO Rick Rioboli Sits at The Center of an Innovation Ecosystem." *Forbes.* October 7, 2019. https://www.forbes.com/sites/peterhigh/2019/10/07/comcast-cio-rick-rioboli-sits-at-the-center-of-an-innovation-ecosystem/?sh=91fc31757fa6.

Lum, Carolyn, and Jakob Brix Danielsen. "Lean Transformation: Eight Tips from Philips." Planet Lean. November 7, 2019. https://planet-lean.com/philips-lean-transformation/.

Planview. "Agile vs Lean." Accessed February 21, 2021. https://www.planview.com/resources/articles/agile-vs-lean/.

Rudder, Carla. "Agile is Ready for its Next Big Break, CIOs Say." *The Enterprisers Project.* August 23, 2018. https://enterprisersproject.com/article/2018/8/agile-ready-its-next-big-break-cios-say.

Rudder, Carla. "Anthem CIO: How Agile Helped Us Drive Value." *The Enterprisers Project.* February 26, 2018. https://enterprisersproject.com/article/2018/2/anthem-cio-how-agile-helped-us-drive-value.

Sigberg, Thorbjørn. "Lean vs Agile vs Lean-Agile." Medium (blog). March 8, 2019. https://medium.com/@thorbjorn.sigberg/lean-vs-agile-vs-lean-agile-c5d38a5406c6.

Tas, Jeroen. "Agile, Lean and the Art of Business—IT Integration." i-CIO. March 2014. https://www.i-cio.com/big-thinkers/jeroen-tas/item/agile-lean-and-the-art-of-business-it-integration.

Chapter 12—Lean of the Future—Hybrid Lean?

A. M. Elmoselhy, Salah. *Hybrid lean-agile manufacturing system technical facet, in automotive sector.* Journal of Manufacturing Systems. Volume 32, Issue 4, 2013. Pages 598-619. https://doi.org/10.1016/j.jmsy.2013.05.011.

Aulinger, Gerd, Mike Rother. "The Role of the Lean Coach." Lean. org. November 2012. https://www.lean.org/coachingkata/Archive.cfm?KataItemId=11#contentTop.

Bailey, Grant. "Office Workers Spend 1,700 Hours a Year in Front of a Computer Screen". *Independent.* July 23, 2018. https://www.independent.co.uk/news/uk/home-news/office-workers-screen-headaches-a8459896.html.

Bradbury, Joel. "What to Know About in Lean Warehouse Management." Industrial Distribution. January 4, 2017. https://www.inddist.com/operations/article/13773359/what-to-know-about-lean-warehouse-management.

Carl. "IOT's Place in the Industry 4.0." Sixfab. July 12, 2018. https://sixfab.com/iots-rise/.

Christie, Brett. "Generation Z's Impact on the Future of Work." Worldatwork. May 31, 2019. https://www.worldatwork.org/workspan/articles/generation-z-impact-s-on-the-future-of-work#.

Customer Insight. "What is 360 Degree Feedback?" Accessed October 31, 2020. https://www.custominsight.com/360-degree-feedback/what-is-360-degree-feedback.asp.

Dave West, and Nigel Thurlow. "Agile Transformation—The Success Story of Scrum & Toyota" Interview transcript from Agile for Automotive Summit, Detroit, MI, May 17, 2019. https://scrumorg-website-prod.s3.amazonaws.com/drupal/2019-02/Final%20-%20Scrum%20and%20Toyota%20Keynote%20Interview%20Spotlight2.pdf.

Kintone. "11 Digital Transformation Quotes to Lead Change and Inspire Action." Medium (blog). May 6, 2019. https://medium.com/digital-transformation-talk/11-digital-transformation-quotes-to-lead-change-inspire-action-a81a3aa79a45.

Krüger, Justus. "Will Industry 4.0 Create a Dark Factory?" Metrology News. March 7, 2019. https://metrology.news/will-industry-4-0-create-the-dark-factory.

Melwin Roy, Dr. Manu. "Lean Leadership." Researchgate. April 2019. https://www.researchgate.net/publication/332275920_Lean_Leadership.

Minter, Steve. "Will Millennials Change Manufacturing?" *Industry Week*. December 28, 2017. https://www.industryweek.com/talent/article/22024832/will-millennials-change-manufacturing.

Null, Christopher. "10 Companies Killing it at Scaling Agile." Techbeacon. October 15, 2020. https://techbeacon.com/app-dev-testing/10-companies-killing-it-scaling-agile.

O'Malley, Thomas. "8 Future Business Trends You Need to Know About." Business.com. December 31, 2016. https://www.business.com/articles/thomas-omalley-future-business-trends.

Ray Nichols, Megan. "RFID and Lean Manufacturing Are a Perfect Pair." Manufacturing.net. March 12, 2018. https://www.manufacturing.net/operations/article/13121578/rfid-and-lean-manufacturing-are-a-perfect-pair.

Stevens, Bill. "The Future of Lean: Four Disruptors of the Decade." Lean Construction Blog. July 2. 2019. https://leanconstructionblog.com/The-Future-of-Lean-Four-Disruptors-of-the-Decade.html.

Chapter 13—Seven Ways Lean Can Evolve

ASQ. "What is the Plan-Do-Check-Act (PDCA) Cycle?" Accessed February 27, 2021. https://asq.org/quality-resources/pdca-cycle.

Buchchols, Scott, and Bill Briggs. *Tech Trends—2020*. Deloitte Insights. January 15, 2020. https://www2.deloitte.com/content/dam/Deloitte/cz/Documents/technology/DI_TechTrends2020.pdf.

Digital Public Library of America. "Golden Age of Radio in the US." Accessed Oct 6, 2020. https://dp.la/exhibitions/radio-golden-age/radio-tv.

Halkias, Maria. "Kroger's New Robotic Warehouse Can Fill a 50-item Order in Less Than 10 Minutes." *The Dallas Morning News*. September 12, 2019. https://www.dallasnews.com/business/retail/2019/09/12/kroger-s-new-robotic-warehouse-can-fill-a-50-item-order-in-less-than-10-minutes.

Kanbanize (blog). "Gemba Walk: Where the Real Work Happens." Accessed February 27, 2021. https://www.kanbanize.com/lean-management/improvement/gemba-walk.

Karimi, Kevyan et al. "Industry 4.0: 7 Real-World Examples of Digital Manufacturing in Action." Autonomous Manufacturing. March 28, 2019. https://amfg.ai/2019/03/28/industry-4-0-7-real-world-examples-of-digital-manufacturing-in-action.

Laaper, Stephen, Brian Kiefer. "Digital Lean Manufacturing: Industry 4.0 Technologies Transform Lean Processes to Advance the Enterprise." Deloitte Insights. August 21, 2020. https://www2.deloitte.com/us/en/insights/focus/industry-4-0/digital-lean-manufacturing.html.

Manyika, James et al. "Help Wanted: The Future of Work in Advanced Economies." McKinsey Global Institute. March 2012. https://www.mckinsey.com/~/media/McKinsey/Featured%20Insights/Employment%20and%20Growth/Future%20of%20

work%20in%20advanced%20economies/Help_wanted_future_
of_work_full_report.pdf.

Mearian, Lucas. "From Coffee Bean to Cup: Starbucks Brews a
Blockchain-based Supply Chain with Microsoft." *Computer
World*. May 7, 2019. https://www.computerworld.com/
article/3393211/from-coffee-bean-to-cup-starbucks-brews-a-
blockchain-based-supply-chain-with-microsoft.html.

Morgan, Blake. "The 10 Most Customer-Obsessed Companies of
2019." *Forbes*. December 20, 2019. https://www.forbes.com/
sites/blakemorgan/2019/12/20/the-10-most-customer-centric-
companies-of-2019/?sh=7e69f03b7a58.

Parekh, Vipul. "Integration of RPA with Blockchain—A Potential New Way to Re-Think Business Models." LinkedIn (blog).
March 20, 2019. https://www.linkedin.com/pulse/integration-
rpa-blockchain-potential-new-way-models-parekh-pmp.

Prabha, Anil. "Are hybrid cloud solutions a win for SMEs?" *TechHQ*.
March 4, 2019. https://techhq.com/2019/03/are-hybrid-cloud-
solutions-a-win-for-smes.

Rudden, Jennifer. "Number of Unicorns Worldwide as of January
2020, by Country." Statista. December 7, 2020.
https://www.statista.com/statistics/1096928/number-of-global-
unicorns-by-country.

Safeatlast. "80 Insightful Internet of Things Statistics (Infographic)."
Infographic. Accessed October 6, 2020. https://safeatlast.co/
blog/iot-statistics.

Stancombe, Christopher. "Tempted to Rewrite Bill Gates' rules on
automation?" Capgemini. January 2, 2015.
https://www.capgemini.com/us-en/2015/01/tempted-to-
rewrite-bill-gates-rules-on-automation.

Taylor, Edward. "VW Deepens Cloud Computing Partnership with
Microsoft." Automotive News. February 27, 2019.

https://www.autonews.com/technology/vw-deepens-cloud-computing-partnership-microsoft.

Think Lean Six Sigma. "What is Gemba and What is its Importance in Lean Manufacturing?" Accessed February 27, 2021. https://thinkleansixsigma.com/article/gemba.

Thota, Narender. "The Rise of RPA in the Manufacturing Industry." VentureIQ. October 16, 2020. https://venturiq.com/insights/the-rise-of-rpa-in-the-manufacturing-industry.

Wexler, Joanie. "Elusive Hybrid Cloud Tops IT Wish Lists." Nutanix. November 30, 2020. https://www.nutanix.com/theforecastbynutanix/technology/elusive-hybrid-cloud-tops-it-wish-lists.

Chapter 14—Conclusion

Goldratt, Eliyahu M. *The Goal: A Process of Ongoing Improvement—25th Anniversary Edition*. Great Barrington—The North River Press, 2012.

Klebnikov, Sergie. "Tesla is Now the World's Most Valuable Car Company with a $208 Billion Valuation." *Forbes*. July 1, 2020. https://www.forbes.com/sites/sergeiklebnikov/2020/07/01/tesla-is-now-the-worlds-most-valuable-car-company-with-a-valuation-of-208-billion/?sh=46ffb87b5334.

Simon Sinek. "The Infinite Game: How to Lead in the 21st Century." May 13, 2019. Video. 1:31:19. https://www.youtube.com/watch?v=3vX2iVIJMFQ.

Made in the USA
Columbia, SC
10 June 2021

39662572R00117